PRAISE FO

I loved this book! UN
moving and wonderf
good girl, I related t.   ... times
when I felt goose-bun   ... and challenged to
go deeper on my own journey to freedom and an
unbound life.

Nicola's writing is raw, honest, true and incredibly
thought-provoking. Thank you for sharing your
gift with us.

Katherine Baldwin, Author of
How to Fall in Love - A 10-Step Journey
to the Heart

I fucking love Nicola Humber! Every time I hear her,
work with her or see her, a fire rises up inside of me;
I'm excited about life and I know I am my true self.

This book is a reflection of that magnificent feeling
- Nicola is our personal mentor and guiding light,
unravelling how we want to feel about ourselves and
handing us the tools and the permission she says we
never needed, to live an unbound life. She gets it.
She gets you.

If, like me, you truly love personal freedom and want
life to be amazing, then I urge you to embark on this
revolutionary and magical journey.

Lyndsey Whiteside
- Starmaker ~ helping you to stand out and
shine!
www.lyndseywhiteside.com

UNBOUND has dramatically expanded my sense of what's possible to create in my life and made me see with fresh eyes how much power I have to follow my own path.

The UNBOUND philosophy rings a clear bell calling all women to embrace their full power. The world needs strong, feminine voices more than ever and I'm so grateful Nicola has gathered all her potent wisdom together in this luscious book.

Leah Kent, Founder of Sacred Unplanning

Being a bound woman is like being a salmon swimming upriver, always fighting the current because of a genetic imperative that seems insurmountable. We struggle with all our might in the wrong direction of the river and at the end, all we have achieved is to spawn and die exhausted. To be UNBOUND is to choose a different fate.

It is to understand that we can overcome our programming and trust the flow of the river.

It is understanding that in the apparent safety of the shallows predators lurk.

It is knowing that if we are ever going fulfil our dream of reaching the sea we must follow the river at its swiftest and trust its flow will help us avoid all potential obstacles and deliver us to a boundless sea where we can grow and thrive and be amazing!

In short for me it is remembering that I am an infinite soul in a finite body and everything is possible if I so choose.

Reading UNBOUND made me feel I can allow myself to grow in any direction I want, I can make my mistakes and own them, learn from them and move on. And best of all it made me feel that by allowing myself to be unbound I can change something in the world.

Chioma Esther Copeman, Founder of Concept Skincare

Reading this book is a magical, healing experience. Within these pages, Nicola guides the reader through the journey of becoming unbound. She doesn't leave you hanging or wanting more, but rather complete - beautifully, unbound and complete. How? Simply by sharing the five principles of living unbound, taking the reader on on a journey through the challenges of becoming unbound, and then providing 6 practices to keep you on the unbound path. This book is mind-blowing, accurate and remarkable.

Thank you, Nicola, for your courage to become unbound, finding a way to put words to the experience, and writing a book to heal women who seek to be unbound. Oh yeah, and also giving us a word for it, unbound!!! You are a light worker!

Tonia Gaudiuso, Financial Intuitive & Organizer

UNBOUND

A guide to walking the unbound path
and becoming your fullest, freest,
most magnificent self

NICOLA HUMBER

For Lou, my soul sister in this and many lifetimes.

UNBOUND: To be free of any old, restrictive
beliefs and stories about
who and how you should be
in the world

To break free of the ties that
have previously bound you

To be your freest, fiercest and
most potently magical self

To live a fully expressed life

A refusal to conform to anyone
else's ideas about how you
live your life

To be fully and most
magnificently you

To be liberated

You do not have to be good.

You do not have to walk on your knees

For a hundred miles through the desert, repenting.

You only have to let the soft animal of your body

love what it loves.

Tell me about your despair, yours, and I will
tell you mine.

Meanwhile the world goes on.

Meanwhile the sun and the clear pebbles of the rain

are moving across the landscapes,

over the prairies and the deep trees,

the mountains and the rivers.

Meanwhile the wild geese, high in the clean blue air,

are heading home again.

Whoever you are, no matter how lonely,

the world offers itself to your imagination,

calls to you like the wild geese, harsh
and exciting —

over and over announcing your place

in the family of things.

WILD GEESE by Mary Oliver

Dear UNBOUND woman,

Thank you so much for picking up a copy of this book (or downloading it to your e-reader). I deeply appreciate the fact that you are intrigued and curious enough to begin this exploration into the idea of unbound.

I want you to know that this is a book I couldn't not write. It comes directly from my heart to yours. Why did I feel compelled to write it? Well for the first 38 years of my life I was living a bound life. I was living a life based on what I perceived was expected of me. And this was a half-life. It was okay, at times it could be great, but it wasn't fully mine.

I squashed myself down.

I modified myself.

I monitored whatever I said or did.

I judged and censored myself.

I held back and kept myself as small as possible.

And no-one would have particularly known this.

On the outside I looked successful, happy and well-functioning.

But I knew.

I knew that I was shrivelling up inside.

Becoming dry.

Brittle.

Liable to shatter.

And a part of me, deep inside, always yearning to be fully expressed; to be fully alive.

I'm writing this book because I don't want that for you.

I've spent the last nine years journeying back to the true me. I know the idea of 'finding yourself' is a total cliché, but I believe we're all here to recognise and return to the fullest, most brilliant, playful, wild and magnificent beings we were when we came into this world.

That's what this book is about.

My intention is to help you unbind yourself from all the conscious and unconscious conditioning you've taken on throughout your life that has told you who and how you should be in the world.

No-one knows you like you do.

And I know you can feel your truest self deep inside. She's there, isn't she?

If you take a moment and get quiet, you can sense her right now.

Your Unbound Self.

During these pages I want to help you reconnect with her.

She might not be completely what you expect. (In fact, I'm pretty sure she won't be). She may challenge you, push your buttons and cause you to question things you have long held dear.

The unbound path is a heroine's journey.

But if you're brave enough (and I have a feeling you are), I invite you to come with me now.

I'm honoured to be your guide and fellow traveller on this journey.

Let's begin.

Nicola x

The unbound woman knows to the core of her being that she is fucking magnificent.

TABLE OF CONTENTS

Praise For Unbound I

Introduction... 1

   The Unbound Self.. 4

   The Half Life 6

   Warning!.. 12

Part One The 5 Principles Of Living Unbound 13

   Principle One - Pleasure... 17

      The Great Switch-Off 19

      The Pleasure Paradox.. 21

      The Path To Pleasure 23

      Magical Manifesting... 25

      The Practice Of Pleasure 29

   Principle Two - Cycles 35

      Medicating Our Magic 37

      The Cyclical Life.. 39

      A Note On Consistency 41

      The Myth Of Lazy 44

   Principle Three - Gift... 51

      Finding 'It' 53

      Moving Into The Gift Zone.................................. 55

      But What Do They Want?................................... 56

      Lesson One: The Difference Between Being In And
Outside Your Gift Zone Can Be Super-Subtle........... 59

      Lesson Two: You Don't Have To
Have It All Figured Out 61

      Lesson Three: What Comes Easily
To You Has The Most Value 63

   Principle Four - Sisterhood 67

      The Myth That You Need To Sacrifice Your Own
Needs To Support Other Women............................. 70

The Myth That Other Women
Are Our Competition 73
The Myth That Being In Sisterhood
Will Get Me Killed 76

Principle Five - Shadow 81
The Shadow Work Of The Body 85
My Left Ear 87
And What Else? 90
Deeply Flawed 91
Over To You 93

Part Two The Challenges Of Living Unbound 95
The Bound Self 101
Sitting In The Void 109
The Unexpected Guilt Of Freedom 115
Radical Responsibility 121
Holding The Paradox 127

Part Three High Potency Practices
For Living Unbound 133
Practice One - Deep Agreement 137
Practice Two - Divine Discipline 145
Practice Three - Conscious Secret Keeping 153
Practice Four - Sacred Boundaries 159
Practice Five - Learning To Listen To Your Body . 167
Practice Six - Conscious Binding 175

Afterword 181

A Prayer For The Unbound Woman 185

Unbound Resources 187

Acknowledgements 189

About The Author 191

INTRODUCTION

When I wrote my first book, Heal Your Inner Good Girl, in 2016, I thought that would be it for a while. I always knew I would write more books. When I was a little girl, I'd dreamed of being a writer and now here I was, doing what I loved, what I was here to do. Still, I was pretty sure that the next book wouldn't come for a while. But as I reached the end of 2016, a new book started to call to me. It was like finding out you're pregnant again when you're still dealing with the sleepless nights, wonder and exhaustion of a new baby. I didn't feel ready to write another book. I had barely been able to appreciate and integrate the first one. But here it was, knocking on my door relentlessly. A book that excited me, even though I couldn't quite pin it down. A book that would be called, simply, UNBOUND.

Why unbound?

Well, this is a word I've been building a relationship with for a while now. Unbound first came calling as I worked through Danielle LaPorte's Desire Map process for the first time and started tuning into my core desired feelings.

How did I want to feel?

Words like free and bold and vibrant and rich came to me, but none of them felt completely compelling. So, I started to dive deeper, looking at the definitions and synonyms for the initial words I had chosen. And that's how I came across unbound. I think it must have been as I was looking up 'free' in a thesaurus. Unbound. Something stirred as I saw the word on the page. I looked up the definition.

UNBOUND: not bound or tied up

not controlled or influenced
by something

not having a cover or binding

'Not having a cover or binding'. Something awakened within me as I read that.

I could feel this word in every cell in my body. Unbound is similar to free, but with the acknowledgement, the knowing, that something has previously been bound, that one has worked to break free, that a process has occurred. And the feeling of freedom is *so* much sweeter because one has previously felt restricted, limited, boxed in, bound.

If you've read Heal Your Inner Good Girl (and my letter to you at the beginning of this book), you'll know that I spent the first forty or so years of my life feeling bound.

Bound by the stories I was telling myself.

Bound by the expectations I imagined that others had of me.

Bound by the role I had agreed to play within my family and friendships and workplaces.

Bound by the 'tyranny of shoulds' and 'musts' and 'ought tos'.

Bound by my limited perception of what was possible for me.

So, the word unbound immediately resonated with me. And I'm imagining it does with you too, as you've picked up this book.

I think it's important to acknowledge here that as a white, Western woman, I certainly haven't experienced the level of bound-ness that many other women have dealt with in the past and are dealing with at this time. However, I didn't want to let this stop me writing this book. Unbound will mean something different to each woman who reads this and we each have our own unique unbinding process. My intention is to give you insights and tools that will help you with yours.

The Unbound Self

When I wrote Heal Your Inner Good Girl, I talked about the Unbound Self - the you who is limitless, free, the fullest expression of who you were born to be. When I started to write about the Unbound Self, I imagined that mine would be full of light, expansive and joyful. However, when I went into meditation to connect with her, I was surprised to find that my Unbound Self was dark and witchy and fierce and fast-moving, full of rage and uncontrollable. Looking back, I don't know why I was surprised. Because what else would the Unbound Self be other than a reflection of the parts of us we've pushed down, suppressed and tried to keep hidden? But still, I was shocked. And I found my Unbound Self very uncomfortable to be with. I was much more comfortable with my Inner Good Girl, the familiar part of me that likes to fit in, get it right and please others.

But here I was, confronted by this wild, rage-y, elemental being who was clearly more than a little pissed off that I had been keeping her quiet for all those years.

Hmmmm. What to do? Put a lid on her and go back to paying lip service to being unbound? Or decide to get to know my Unbound Self better? To give her space. To listen to her. To feel her.

To be honest, I spent the first few months after connecting with my Unbound Self swinging between the two. I was just playing at being unbound; letting the lid off a little and then trying to squeeze her back into the box. And it was pretty darn frustrating. Because once I had connected with my Unbound Self, it was impossible to un-know her. I could always feel her presence bubbling away underneath, especially when I was trying to do things 'properly' and find the 'right' way. That's when she rose up, like a lioness, causing me to sabotage my good girl efforts and leaving me with unexpected (and often unwanted) ideas and feelings. I realised that my Unbound Self couldn't be un-listened to.

And this is the challenge. Because we're conditioned to live in a bound way. We're brought up to follow certain rules (which are often unspoken, but deeply engrained). We're rewarded for fitting in, by our families, our teachers and society in general. And it can feel so much easier to live in a way that feels structured, with a rhythm and routine that's familiar. Even at times when we're frustrated with the way things are in our lives, there's something soothing in the knowledge that each day will pretty much be the same as the last. Yes, we might make changes. We meet new people. We travel to new places. We choose a new job. We try a new activity. But these changes tend to be the exception rather than the norm. And once the change has been made, homeostasis ensures that we quickly settle back into a comfortable routine.

The Half Life

The numbing comfort of the familiar is the reason why most of us end up living a half-life; a dry existence of people-pleasing and trying to fit in. There's a part of us that just wants to stay safe, so when we get the idea to change careers or leave a restrictive relationship or share our truth with the world, although the Unbound Self might be calling us forward, that safety-seeking part holds us back.

Think about your future.

Better the devil you know.

Don't rock the boat.

All of these well-meaning statements keep us stuck in the half-life. And it can feel okay. We tick along, maybe we even experience moments of joy, but mostly we don't feel fully alive.

I think back to when I went travelling for six months in my mid-thirties. I took a sabbatical from my secure job in finance and went off to visit three of the countries I'd always wanted to go to - Peru, Australia and India. I lived with a local family in Cusco and learned Spanish, I flew over the Nazca Lines, did conservation voluntary work in Queensland, saw an opera at the Sydney Opera House, worked with children in a nursery at a temple in Northern India and trekked in the foothills of the Himalayas. It was an extraordinary experience. Truly unbound. And after six months when I returned home I imagined that I'd be changed forever. I was excited to tell friends and family about my travels. But of course, life had continued as normal for the people I'd left behind for those six months. Although they were pleased to see me and wanted to hear about all I'd been up to on my travels, within a couple of days that excitement had died down. And I slipped back into my 'old' life; the half-life. I returned to my job. I went out to the same places. I fell back into a deeply unsuitable relationship. In many ways it felt like nothing had changed.

I thought back to people I'd met on my trip, people of a similar age to me who'd gone travelling to find themselves, to discover that 'something' they felt was missing, to find out what they were meant to be doing with their lives. I wondered how they felt once they got home. Some of them had given up jobs, sold property, left relationships, to go on a journey of discovery. I remember speaking to one woman who was coming to the end of her trip and hearing a sense of panic in her voice because she hadn't found what she'd been looking for. She still had no idea what she wanted to do with her life. What the fuck? She felt betrayed. Betrayed by that unbound part of her that called upon her to go halfway across the world on what she now saw as a fruitless search. And I hate to admit that as I spoke to her, a part of me felt a smug sense of satisfaction. I told myself that I'd had no such expectations. I was purely here for the experience. I had a job and a home to return to. Lucky me. But of course, that meant that I easily slipped back into the familiar way of life I'd left behind; a bound way of life. So much for smug satisfaction!

Looking back I can see that this is not 100% true. Because, although I fell back into the welcoming arms of the familiar, things were never quite the same after that six months away. Something had awakened in me. And within two years I'd left my job and decided to retrain as a coach and hypnotherapist.

And this is the thing, unbound is not a one-off happening. It's a process. We unbind ourselves from old, restrictive patterns, beliefs and stories over a period of time. Healing the Inner Good Girl is just the beginning. The journey to becoming truly unbound is a long one with many challenges. The path spirals round again and again, and you find yourself revisiting the same issues from a different angle, each time unlocking a new piece of the puzzle.

My intention with this book is to be your guide on the journey to becoming unbound, to help you clear the way, to flag up the potential obstacles and to show you some magical diversions. (I was tempted to write 'short-cuts' then, but there are no real short-cuts to becoming unbound. This is a journey to be savoured, with many unexpected twists and turns).

I'm not going to sugar-coat it; your Unbound Self will demand a lot from you as you walk this new path. She doesn't do half-measures. She's not the kind of gal who dips her toe into the water.

She dives right in.

Naked.

With a roar of delight.

And she will expect you to join her whole-heartedly.

Because she's been waiting a long time.

For you.

Are you ready?

Come on. Let's do this together.

I've been walking the unbound path for a while now and I'd love to be your guide. In the pages of this book, I'll share the principles of living unbound. These are the keys that will unlock the door to your own, unique unbound life. Each one on its own is powerful. When you combine these principles together, they are like your own personal Kryptonite.

I'll help you to recognise and shift the old patterns that have been keeping you stuck in the familiarity of the half-life, a place that can feel comfortable, whilst also deeply restricting your ability to be your fullest, most magical self.

We'll explore the unique challenges that come with being unbound and how to recognise these challenges as ways to actually increase your personal power.

I'll take you to meet the part of you that actually takes pleasure from limitation, the Bound Self. She is just as, if not more magical, than your Unbound Self and I'll help you to make her an ally, rather than a hidden enemy.

And I'll help you to tune into the practices that will enable you to maintain a state of high potency. Because this is what's required from an unbound woman.

You are a map-maker, not a follower.

You are a powerful creator, not a consumer.

If you're reading this book, know that you're one of the pioneers who is blazing a trail and creating new ways to be in the world. This means that you need to feel deeply supported and the high-potency practices I share in the final part of this book will help you with that.

We'll begin with the five principles of living unbound.

The unbound woman goes first.

WARNING!

Do not proceed beyond this point unless you are willing to experience profound transformation in all areas of your life.

Side effects of walking the unbound path can include:

- Making radical (and often uncomfortable) changes
- Speaking your truth and finding your roar
- Pissing off people who are stuck in the half life
- Being thought of as crazy, strange or just plain weird
- Standing out and attracting attention
- Increased levels of uncertainty

You must be willing to sit with the unfamiliar, commit to listening to the deepest wishes of your Unbound Self and to act on the whispers of your soul.

You will be called upon to go first, to be courageous and bring your full self to a world that's not quite ready for you.

If you're willing to accept all of this, the rewards can be great.

Are you ready to go deeper?

PART ONE

THE 5 PRINCIPLES OF LIVING UNBOUND

The unbound woman allows pleasure to be her compass.

PRINCIPLE ONE - PLEASURE

The first principle of living unbound is to allow pleasure to be your compass; to do what feels good and to be guided by your desire. Sounds easy, doesn't it? Let's move on to the next chapter then...

But wait just a minute, the truth is that following your pleasure is not as simple as it seems. In fact, it can be mighty challenging.

Why so?

Well on a day-to-day basis most of us have no real clue what brings us true pleasure. Now you may question this statement, but if I were to ask you now, 'What do you really want?' (And I mean *really*), would you be able to answer with certainty?

Maybe you could let me know some things that would give you a temporary lift: a fresh cup of coffee, a walk in nature, a massage. But when we get to the bigger question of 'How do you really want your life to be?', then things can start to get cloudier. Because the stakes are higher.

How you want your life to be, who you want to surround yourself with (and how you want those relationships to be), what you want to create and how you want to spend your time, are all big questions. And being brave enough to listen to the answers, then make changes based upon them, can lead to huge repercussions.

That's why most of us don't listen. Or we wait until things get unbearable before finally deciding to say, 'Fuck it!' and go for what we really want in our lives.

(And I'm certainly talking from personal experience here. I put up with chronic dissatisfaction for many years before deciding to consciously create the life I really wanted).

But there's another reason why many of us are not able to be guided by pleasure. And that is the fact that most women have been conditioned to completely disconnect from their desire.

From a very early age, girls are taught to put other peoples' needs above their own and to suppress their wants. They're told that it's wrong to ask for what you want ('Askers don't get' is one of the most limiting statements there is) and that no-one likes a girl who's enjoying herself too much ('Who does she think she is?') And, perhaps most destructively, girls receive the message that it's dirty to receive pleasure from their bodies.

The Great Switch-Off

I remember when I was very young (maybe three or four years old), I discovered that I could generate a huge amount of pleasure from lying on my front and grinding my hand against my 'foo foo' (as I then called it). For a couple of blissful evenings, I positioned myself half underneath the sofa and half outside and had a wonderful time rubbing myself with abandon.

I couldn't believe that I'd found something that felt so good! Hours of pleasure awaited.

But after a couple of nights of this, my parents put a stop to it. I'm not sure what they said to me, but I received the message loud and clear that what I was doing was wrong, dirty and somehow shameful.

I was confused. How could something that felt so good be so wrong?

Of course, I was far too young to articulate this question. I picked up on my parents' embarrassment and took my rubbing undercover. It always felt somehow dirty after that though; something I needed to hide and do in secret. And from that point, I began years of mistrusting my body. Because I'd got the message that just because I received pleasure from something didn't mean it was right. In fact, it could be very wrong. Others might judge or criticise me. So, I needed to carefully monitor what I did to feel good. I needed to stick within acceptable limits. And I didn't get to choose what was acceptable.

I don't blame my parents for this. Because, let's face it, we're all confused when it comes to pleasure and desire. We all receive conflicting messages from the people around us, the media and society in general about what's acceptable. And here they were with a little girl who'd suddenly taken to self-pleasuring every evening right there in their living room. To be honest, I'm not sure I'd have handled things too differently.

The sad truth is although you come into the world as a being who is completely plugged into what you want, you very quickly begin to shut off from your desires. You question what feels good and start to mistrust your own body. Many of our desires get judged as wrong and pushed down into the unconscious where they can and do wreak havoc in later life (much more on this in later in the book).

As we grow older, this sense of disconnection becomes more strategic - we numb ourselves with food, alcohol, drugs, social media, TV and over-work. Life becomes one big distraction.

And that's the key. Because in order to follow your desire, you need to be fully present. And honestly, how often does that happen?

The Pleasure Paradox

The pleasure paradox is one that is particularly key for women, because it just so happens that each of us have been given a very special part of the body that's designed only to give pleasure; the clitoris. This magical organ has 8000 nerve endings (double the nerve endings in the glans of the penis) and it has no other function than to generate pleasure. So, of course, when I discovered this as a little girl, although I had no name for it, I was delighted. I thought I'd won the jackpot! But very soon I learned that it was somehow wrong to access this pleasure that was so very readily available.

Huh? What the actual fuck?

You can see the conflict here, can't you? As women we're uniquely designed to experience great amounts of pleasure.Yet at the same time, from a very young age, we're also taught that it's wrong to do so.

No wonder we get so completely disconnected from our desires.

Because of this we tend to stick within those deadening, 'acceptable' limits when it comes to our choices about what feels good. We forget what we really want.

It's time to remember.

In fact, as an unbound woman you have a duty to yourself and the collective to reconnect with your desire, to rediscover what really turns you on.

The truth is that by making a commitment to rediscover your pleasure and reconnect with your Unbound Self, the shifts you experience as an individual will also impact all beings. The impact of any changes you make will ripple out into the collective consciousness. So, you're doing this work not just for yourself, but for every single person on the planet.

The Unbound Woman knows that personal liberation
is the first step on the path to freedom for the collective.

No pressure.

Seriously, I don't want you to see this as a pressure, something you're obligated to do. My desire (see what I did there?) is to activate a greater, deeper sense of purpose within you.

Sometimes we're willing to do things for others that we're not willing to do for ourselves.

So, when things become challenging on this path (and they will), know that you're not just doing this for you. You're also doing this to create freedom in the collective. Let the power of that move you onwards.

The Path to Pleasure

The best way to reconnect with your desire is to start listening deeply to your body. Because she will always let you know what is going to give you pleasure (if you allow her to).

As a general rule, if something gives you real pleasure your body will open, soften, relax, enliven and juicify.

In contrast, if something is not truly in your pleasure zone, your body will constrict, stiffen, tense up, become numb and dry.

(And I'm not just talking about sexual pleasure here).

The path to pleasure is very clear if you allow it to be. But most of us have been putting up with a numb, dry, half-life for a long, long time, so the sensations of desire have become completely unfamiliar (and even uncomfortable).

I invite you to get to know your pleasure again.

Why is this so important? Well when we're disconnected from our desire, everything we manifest in our lives is coming from a limited (bound) place. When you don't really know what you want, how can you create it?

So instead we unconsciously look at what others have got and decide that maybe we want that too?

We listen to others when they tell what we *should* want.

We get sucked in by ads that tell us that we want more stuff.

We get brainwashed by books and programmes that convince us we need to be somehow different.

We get lost in a sea of confusion and mixed messages, and manifesting from that place is anything but potent.

It suits the current system we live in, the patriarchy, for us to be disconnected from our desire and confused about what we really want. Because if we did allow ourselves to know and follow our pleasure, we'd each become truly powerful.

Your pleasure is your power source.

And your Unbound Self communicates with you via your desires. If you want something, if you have a true desire for it, know that this is no accident. When you begin to feel a stirring of desire, this is your Unbound Self letting you know that this is your next step. But so often we ignore her call. We tell ourselves we can't have what we want, that it's too much, or the wrong thing, or it doesn't make sense.

What if you truly listened to your desires and allowed pleasure, rather than logic to guide you?

Magical Manifesting

Think for a moment. Can you remember a time in the past when you were trying to manifest something because deep down you felt you should? This want didn't come from a place of desire, but instead from a feeling of wanting to prove yourself, to keep up and fit in.

What happened?

I can pretty much guarantee that it was bloody hard work and if you did manage to create this thing, you experienced a feeling of anti-climax and dissatisfaction afterwards.

Now, think about a time when you were manifesting from a place of pure pleasure. This might be trickier to remember an example of because we're conditioned to create logically from our heads, rather than the deep knowing of our bodies. But I'm sure there have been times in the past when you've allowed yourself to be guided by your true wants.

What happened? I can imagine that your desire manifested with surprising ease.

When we're trying to figure out what we want with our minds, it's all too easy to get caught up in 'shoulds' and comparing and distraction. We manifest from a restricted place of what we imagine is possible, based on what we've experienced in the past, what we've been told and what we've seen others create.

This place is deeply UN-magical.

By encouraging you to reconnect with your pleasure, I'm inviting you to get out of your head and into your body. Whenever you do this, you move out of your own way. You simply focus on what feels good and your Unbound Self has the freedom she's been waiting for. She starts to draw your true desires to you. And often these are things you didn't even know you wanted on a conscious level.

But when these opportunities, people and places appear in your life, you just know they are right for you. You feel a sense of expansion, a quickening; you feel elevated.

This is magical.

I've experienced this myself time and time again.

Before I met my now husband, I had been trying to find a true partner for many years. I'd been operating from my head, imagining what I thought I was possible for me. (And this seemed to be either someone 'nice' but not particularly compelling, or someone exciting and charismatic, who I wasn't able to trust). After two particularly destructive relationships, I had been through a period of online dating, which turned out to be both depressing and disheartening.

So, I took a step back. I realised that I was happy with my single life. I had a lovely home, I'd recently made the decision to change direction and retrain as a coach and hypnotherapist, I had wonderful friends and I felt fulfilled. I decided to focus on the life I did have and allowing that to be as pleasurable as possible.

Without really knowing it, I got out of my own way.

And within a few months, I received a Facebook message out of the blue from Mark, a boy I'd been at school with back in the eighties (and who I'd had a HUGE crush on). I hadn't seen him since we'd left school over twenty years before, so when he randomly got in touch it felt magical.

We'd both been on our own paths, enjoying full lives and challenges along the way, travelling, working, learning, and when we came together in our late thirties we were both at a stage where we felt ready to have a committed relationship.

If we'd met at any time in the previous twenty years, I'm pretty sure our relationship wouldn't have worked out. One or the other of us would have been with someone else, we would have been in different geographical locations or we just wouldn't have got on. But now, here was this man I was very attracted to (tick!) who was also deeply kind, funny, intelligent, confident, accepting and so much more (including incredibly challenging at times!).

I couldn't have imagined the kind of relationship we have if I'd been operating from my head. The truth was I had all kinds of stories running about what was possible for me. But because I'd allowed myself to drop into my pleasure zone, my Unbound Self was able to manifest a magical partner for me.

This kind of thing happens with my clients over and over again. They come to work with me because they think they want something, but once I help them to move out of their logical thinking and reconnect with their deep inner knowing, their Unbound Selves are able to show them what they truly desire and draw it towards them.

The Practice of Pleasure

Knowing and following your pleasure is a practice. What I mean by that is this isn't something you think about once and start doing immediately. This is a process of checking in continually with everything you do and asking 'Is this going to bring me pleasure in some way? Is this what I *truly* desire or am I doing this because I feel I should?'

Truth Talk: If you find yourself saying or thinking 'should' at any time, it's a sign you're wandering off the unbound path. We all have obligations in life, but sometimes we create extra obligations because we're following the expected path, rather than going in the direction of what we really want.

Allowing pleasure to be your compass takes bravery because it's not necessarily going to lead you where you thought you were going to go. It requires you to question *everything* in your life and there may be things that you need to let go of, both big and small. It requires you to ask whether the things that you have in your life already are the things that you *truly* desire. This can take you in very unexpected directions. The idea of following your bliss is a relatively easy concept to grasp, but it's not so easy to actually integrate that into your life. The key here is to listen to your body.

As you read this book, you'll realise (or rather remember) that your body is your biggest source of wisdom. I'll be inviting you to return to her time and time again in these pages. And particularly when it comes to knowing what gives you pleasure, your body is going to be your greatest guide.

Within the bonus resources for this book, you'll find a guided meditation designed to help you reconnect with your body and access her wisdom.

Access these free resources at:

nicolahumber.com/unbound-resources

In addition to this powerful meditation, here are some journaling questions to help you reflect on the ways you've been encouraged to shut your desire down in the past and reawaken your connection with your pleasure.

Take some time to journal on the following questions:

What was I told about pleasure/having fun/enjoying myself when I was a child?

What messages did I receive about my body and feeling pleasure in my body?

What experiences have I had where I was freely enjoying myself and then something or someone shut me down in some way?

How did I see the people around me experiencing pleasure when I was growing up? Were there any negative consequences/costs to this (either to themselves or others)?

In what ways do I numb/distract myself rather than listening to the wisdom of my body?

What is stopping me from being fully in my pleasure right now?

Complete the following statements. (Don't think too much about this or monitor yourself. Just allow the words to flow):

Pleasure is ......

My desire is ......

When I enjoy myself other people ......

When a women feels good she ......

If I were to allow myself to truly follow my pleasure I would ......

My body is ......

When I see another woman who is completely in her pleasure I ......

When you recognise and embody your true nature as an unbound woman, you access an unlimited source of power within you.

PRINCIPLE TWO - CYCLES

The next principle of living unbound is to know and harness the power of your cyclical nature. As a woman you experience and are influenced by many different cycles, some of which include:

- Your menstrual cycle (if you have one)
- The cycle of the moon
- The cycle of the seasons
- Your creative cycle
- The cycle of each day
- Your life-cycle

In addition to these, each of your relationships, projects and activities have a cyclical rhythm to them.

But the world we live in does not encourage or allow us to honour these different cycles. We're conditioned to believe that life happens in a linear, step-by-step, one thing after another way. It does not.

Our education system and workplaces tend to have rigid structures that don't allow in any way for the natural ebb and flow of our energies.

We're taught that we should be continually moving forward, and that progress happens in a cumulative way. This is a myth.

Life is cyclical.

All beings on this planet are cyclical, particularly women. And this is one of our gifts.

But instead of being treasured, our cyclical nature has been trampled on.

Trying to stay within a 9-5, Monday to Friday working week is deadening to the unbound woman.

The expectation of constantly being in action exhausts us.

The idea that we should be emotionally 'level' and that any mood swings are a cause for concern suppresses us.

Medicating our Magic

This ignorance towards and dismissal of our inherent cyclical nature has reached such epidemic proportions that many women volunteer to medicate themselves in order to avoid the natural ups and downs of their experience.

I took the pill injection for a number of years in my late thirties and early forties. This was primarily for contraceptive purposes, but I saw the fact that I wouldn't have periods whilst having the pill injection as a benefit. I was happy to avoid what I saw as the inconvenient swings in my emotional state and the monthly messiness of menstruation. At the time I had no idea that the menstrual cycle is actually an immense source of power as a woman, or that the changes in my emotions were important signals about what was happening in my life and my relationship to those events. I believed that I should feel level and any emotional outburst was a sign there was something wrong with me.

And quite honestly just reading what I've written in the last paragraph infuriates me, because I'd been brainwashed with this patriarchal, preposterous idea about what was 'normal' and spent years suppressing my true nature accordingly.

It's only when I started to come into contact with the work of incredible teachers like Lisa Lister and Miranda Gray that I realised I'd been completely hoodwinked. I read 'The Pill. Are You Sure It's for You?' by Jane Bennett and Alexandra Pope and decided immediately to stop having pill injections. As my natural rhythms returned, I realised how numb I'd been during the years I'd been taking it. It was as if I'd been living in this grey fog; nothing had seemed particularly bad, but I'd been disconnected from my joy as well.

I had made the choice to start having the pill injection at a time of my life when I would have said I was pretty self-aware and connected with my body. If anyone had asked, I would have told them I was well-informed. But the fact is I'd never questioned the idea of taking a hormonal contraceptive and I'd certainly never thought to question whether it really was 'normal' for us to be feel emotionally and energetically consistent.

So, I wonder how many women are falling for these insidious constructs?

How many women are being energetically and emotionally muzzled in this way?

How many women are being made to feel wrong for the way they naturally are?

The Cyclical Life

I'm not just talking about our menstrual cycles here. As women, our energies ebb and flow with the waxing and waning of the moon. We feel quite differently depending on what season it is, naturally wanting to slow down, retreat and rest in the darker days of winter and moving into creative action and momentum as we journey into spring and summer.

If we allow it, we experience ourselves and our lives quite differently at the various stages of our life. And each project we work on has distinct stages, as we move from awareness to idea, to planning, to action, to completion, to integration, to reflection and into the void; the in-between place that we naturally retreat to after a cycle of action.

But the only stages of these cycles that are valued in society are those that involve action. We're encouraged to be doing all the time and made to feel wrong if we want and need to slow down and rest.

We're told that we should carry on as usual during our periods, when really our bodies are craving retreat at this time and are open to deep, intuitive wisdom.

Each January we're cajoled to make resolutions and big plans for the year, regardless of the fact that this is still mid-winter in the northern hemisphere.

And the younger stages of life, the maiden and the mother, tend to be valued over the older stages of the enchantress and the crone. We're distracted from the power and wisdom we can access and embody as we move into our forties, fifties and beyond by a conditioned need to look younger and put up with retreating into the background and becoming invisible.

Well, quite frankly, fuck that!

The unbound woman honours every part of the different, unique cycles of her life. She commits to becoming more and more aware of how her energies shift at different times. She's curious about how she feels super-inspired on some days, like a decision-making, action-taking boss on others and craves rest and peacefulness at other times. She relishes every single stage of her life; rather than dreading the ageing process, she welcomes it as an opportunity to step more fully into her unbound wisdom.

I invite you to move more deeply into your cyclical nature.

A Note on Consistency

I want to mention here how harnessing the power of your cyclical nature relates to consistency. When I asked the women in my online community about what stopped them feeling fully expressed in their lives, some mentioned that they didn't feel able to make the kind of progress that they would like, because they weren't able to maintain consistent levels of action.

I could identify with this. Consistency is always held up as a key factor when it comes to creating success in any field (whatever 'success' means, but that's a whole other conversation!). But I had always struggled to be consistent in the typical sense, even when doing things that I loved, like writing and growing my business. For many years, I beat myself up about this. Maybe I was just lazy? (More on the myth of 'lazy' in a while). Maybe there was something wrong with me? Why couldn't I keep a consistent momentum going?

I finally had an a-ha moment during an interview with witch and menstrual maven, Lisa Lister. As we were speaking about this very topic - consistency - she mentioned that, as a woman, you need to give yourself permission to be inconsistent.

My inner good girl thought, 'Whaaat? That can't be right'. But my Unbound Self recognised this as deep and ancient wisdom.

The fact is that as women we're not designed to be consistent.

We're designed to be cyclical.

So, yes, an element of consistency is important, but it needs to be integrated within our cyclical nature. It's no good thinking that we can just be rigidly consistent and do the same things day in and day out, that we can be constantly in action mode. If we simply relate consistency to action then we're setting ourselves up for failure, because it's going to be impossible for us to sustain in the long-term. We might be able to sustain consistency for a period of time, but at some point (and often sooner than we think), we will move out of alignment and it will lead to burnout.

What I encourage my unbound clients to do, and what I do for myself, is a practice of consistent inconsistency (or inconsistent consistency). This means acknowledging you're not a rigidly consistent being and recognising there will be times of the day, month and year when you feel like you want to be in action, times when you feel more creative and like you want to be out in the world connecting with others. And there will be other times when you want to retreat inwards. All of these stages are just as valuable as the others.

It's also important and freeing to realise that there will be times when you feel like everything's falling apart! You will go through phases which may well feel quite destructive and that's all part of the normal cycle of your life. These are times of upheaval, of clearing, of letting go, of making space. These are times of coming back to who you are. But again, we're taught to resist these falling apart times, to fear them and try and pull ourselves back together as quickly as possible. When you're able to recognise these as the transformational spaces they actually are, you can be fully in your unbound power.

When we begin to relate consistency to our cyclical nature, it makes more sense and it gives us permission to really harness the times when we feel like we do want to be in action and we are feeling very creative. Also, we're able to recognise the times when we feel like we want to retreat and rest and restore, and give ourselves permission to do just that.

The Myth of Lazy

I've heard many women call themselves out as lazy over the years. Whether it's my mentoring clients guiltily sharing how they feel they *should* be doing more or acquaintances posting online to declare that one of their blocks is pure laziness, I've heard the 'lazy' tag over and over again.

I have a personal history with the word 'lazy' and it used to trigger me hugely. I've been called lazy in the past and it has cut me to the quick. Because at the time, I secretly feared that I really *was* lazy. In fact, at my darkest times I would imagine myself as this disgusting, slimy slug-like creature. I had huge shame around the fact that I didn't want to be working super-hard or filling every hour of my day with activity. For many years I felt like there was something wrong with me.

In my bound life I spent many years working 9-5 in a variety of corporate environments. And because I would get up every day to go and sit in an office, I had the perfect defence against being called lazy.

I would show up to work. I would be physically present.

Therefore, I was seen (and saw myself) as productive and consistent.

But in my time as a seemingly productive member of society, there were many days when I would sit at my desk, pushing paper around whilst internally despairing at the mind-numbing drudgery of it all.

And every now and then, I would be unable to make myself go into the office, because that feeling of despair would overtake me. These were dark days.

But amidst the darkness and despair, at least I could convince myself I wasn't lazy. Because I had a J.O.B.

Then when I left the corporate world and started my own business, suddenly I had the time-freedom I had craved for so long. But when I started my coaching and hypnotherapy practice, one of my very first thoughts was, 'How should I fill all of this time?' (In other words, 'Shit! How do I maintain the illusion of busy-ness and productivity now I have all this freedom?')

Starting with the main intention of filling my time meant that for the first couple of years in my business I worked more hours than I had ever done in my 9-5. And this wasn't because I had to. It was because I chose to.

I chose to work all the hours because I didn't want to appear lazy. What if people found out that I was actually this disgusting, sluggish creature who infinitely preferred afternoon naps to hustling?

So, I created endless (and often meaningless) tasks because I wanted to look productive.

And eventually I burned out. What's worse is the fact that I burned out even though my business wasn't successful at the time. I was barely making ends meet. After all those hours I'd put in!

Something wasn't right.

Because I wasn't the only one. I could see lots of other women around me who had made the bold and beautiful decision to start their own businesses, women who desired freedom and flexibility beyond all else, and those same women were all feeling exhausted, drained and most definitely not lit up or free.

What I eventually realised is that by trying to sustain the hustle, hustle, hustle work ethic, we were completely denying our cyclical nature. We'd been trying to fit into an old, linear, rigidly consistent way of doing things. And that was never going to work.

So many of the women I saw around me were succumbing to burn-out, working themselves into the ground and then beating themselves up because they couldn't take the pace.

So, unbound one, I want to let you know right now, if you've ever judged yourself as lazy or berated yourself for not being able to maintain continual action, it's time to honour and work in alignment with your true nature.

And here are two ways you can get started...

How to harness the power of your cyclical nature

1) For the next 30 days, keep track of your energy levels and desires in a journal. Notice the times when you feel like you want to be in action, times when you want to be creating, times when you want to be with other people and times when you want to retreat. Notice any patterns and how they relate to where you are in your own menstrual cycle and the phase of the moon.

For more information on how to harness the power of your menstrual cycle, I recommend checking out Lisa

Lister's wonderful book, Code Red. And to find out what moon phase we're in at any particular time, go to: timeanddate.com/moon/phases

As you gather this intel on your own cyclical nature, ask yourself, 'What would my days/weeks/months look like if I allowed myself to embody the cyclical, unbound woman I am?' See what answers come to you and give yourself permission to implement at least some of them.

2) Experiment with doing less. Much less. You may have heard of the Pareto principle which, in very basic terms, states that 80% of results come from 20% of actions. What if you allowed yourself to do only 20% of what you usually do? What would you let go of? What are those key activities that harvest the best results for you? What if you stopped doing all of that busy work?

In my experience, an approach of radical non-action can work wonders. Give yourself the space you crave and notice what emerges from that space.

The unbound woman recognises that what she does and what she brings to the world is limitless, luminous and multi-faceted.

PRINCIPLE THREE - GIFT

The third principle of living unbound is to live in and from your gift. What is your gift? Something that you give willingly, something that evokes joy in you as you give it, something that feels deeply natural to you, something that makes you more YOU in the giving of it.

Imagine living in and from that place? That delicious spot where what you bring to the world fills you up and helps the blood of life flow into all the many unique aspects of you.

Yummmmm!

But like all of these principles, living in and from our gifts, being and bringing what we were born to do in the world, is something we've systematically been conditioned not to do. #deepsigh

From very early on in our lives we're shepherded into easily labelled boxes, encouraged to follow a conventional, set path and become a good citizen (aka consumer). We're taught to compare ourselves unfavourably to others, to try and keep up. We're taught that life is a struggle, a slog and you have to work hard. We're told that no-one likes their jobs, so why should you be any different? Put up and shut up. Don't rock the boat and certainly don't get your hopes up. Maybe you can do what you really love when you retire? (If you get to retire).

We're taught that there are certain ways of doing things, of living life, and these usually involve boredom and generally sucking it up. We're taught to suppress our dreams and accept a half-life of drudgery. We're conditioned to believe that we're too much and not good enough all at the same time. (Mind-fuck, anyone?) We're taught that there can't be any value in anything that comes easily. There has to be a catch, so scale back your vision. That will never work. Who do you think you are?

And as all of these stories, judgements and criticisms build up, layer after layer, your gift shrinks away. It falls back into the shadows.

Hiding.

Hiding.

Hiding.

It's time to coax your gift out into the world unbound one, your unique gift, that thing that comes so easily and beautifully to you.

We need it.

Finding 'it'

With all the conditioning we've been subject to, from the time we were very young, it's no wonder the unbound woman can get very confused about what her gift actually is.

When I speak to the women in my online community, often they tell me they want to find their life purpose. They know deep down they're here for something special, something important, but they can't seem to find IT.

This IT is elusive. And you can read books, attend workshops or access the Akashic Records to find your 'life purpose'.

But here's a spoiler alert - your life purpose is simply to be as YOU as you can possibly be.

YOU are the gift.

You don't need to 'do' anything special. Your only mission in this lifetime is to move more deeply into your you-ness. And this is what your Unbound Self is desperate for you to know.

But like all of these principles, this is not as simple as it seems. Because throughout your life you will have picked up a lot of NON-you-ness. So, this is a process of stripping away the non-you and all those things you can do that aren't in your gift zone. Gay Hendricks, author of 'The Big Leap' calls this your Zone of Genius, that place where you become so excited by your mission you can't wait to get out of bed in the morning. It's when you create a life, career or business that is uniquely expressing your true gifts. It's in this place that magic happens.

Moving into the Gift Zone

How do you find your gift zone?

Well, the first step is to stop comparing yourself to others. Comparison-itis is one of the scourges of modern society. The world is set up to get us to compare ourselves to as many other people as possible. Social media, advertisements; it's all designed to make us believe we're not quite 'enough', that we need to be and have more. Positioned as a way of connecting, we're instead continually bombarded with a false reality of other peoples' lives. We see the edited highlight reel of what other people are up to and then beat ourselves up for not being able to attain it for ourselves.

This results in is a huge waste of time and energy trying to strive towards something we're not, moving further and further away from our gifts.

Your Unbound Self has no time for comparison-itis. She knows that you are magnificent. She knows that you already have everything you need, and you are all you need to be. The idea that you would squander precious time comparing yourself to others and judging yourself unfavourably is bizarre to her. 'Come back to yourself!', she calls. She knows you are the gift.

But of course, you've forgotten. And this life is about remembering.

Can you remember?

The first step is to stop looking 'over there'.

But What Do THEY Want?

The next step to moving into your gift zone? To stop asking the question, 'What do THEY want?' Many of life's problems are built upon this question. The amount of time and effort that goes into trying to figure out other peoples' wants.

Your partner.

Your parents.

Your friends.

Your colleagues.

Your potential clients.

'How can I shape myself and what I do to meet their expectations?' Chipping away at your edges, making yourself acceptable, attractive, anodyne, consumable.

What if you simply chose to focus on what YOU want? This is the key to living in and from your gift.

Let me give you an example.

When I first started my hypnotherapy and coaching practice, I had no idea how to run a business. All I knew was that I had a calling to help people, and somewhere underneath that was a desire to journey deeper into myself (although I didn't realise that at the time). So, I started searching for information about how to create a successful business.

One of the pieces of advice that kept coming up was to have a defined niche, to decide exactly who I wanted to help and to get clear on their pain points. 'What keeps your ideal client up at night?', I was asked by various mentors.

So, I decided on a niche - weight loss. And this wasn't based on what I particularly *wanted* to do, or the work I loved doing. I chose it because it was marketable. I knew that people wanted help to lose weight. It's what the majority of my hypnotherapy clients came to me for. I could easily reel off the kind of things that might be keeping my potential clients awake at night. I was all set. I had my niche. And it should have been easy to grow my business from this place. But it wasn't.

I struggled to find clients. I felt hemmed in and restricted. I could create content and programmes, but I wasn't passionate about them. I wasn't in my gift. This wasn't what I was here to do. And my Unbound Self knew it.

Truth talk: If you're not operating from your gift zone, your Unbound Self will keep nudging (or forcing!) you to move towards what you're really here to do.

After a couple of years plugging away at weight loss, I knew that I had to shift focus. And again, the advice to have clear, defined, marketable niche rang in my ears. So, I decided that I would help women business-owners with their money blocks. This was something I'd done a lot of work on myself. I had a background in finance. Tick! And I was passionate about helping women who'd made the courageous decision to start their own businesses to create an abundant income. Double tick!

Surely this was my gift?

Well I was on the right track. Focusing on the niche of money mindset helped me to reach more people and grow my business. But still something was sticking. My business didn't take off in the way I had hoped it would. I wanted to fly, and it still felt like I was tethered in some way.

How could this be? I had all the ticks, but I didn't feel fulfilled, free, or deeply excited about what I was doing.

It's only when I stumbled upon the word 'unbound' that my gift really started to wake up. I didn't know it at the time, but unbound was my way in. It unlocked something within me. This certainly wasn't clear immediately. I spent another couple of years focusing on money mindset (because it made sense), but unbound was always there.

And when I started to write this book, it became clearer. This is what I'm here to do; to help other women to become unbound, as I continue to unbind myself.

As I stepped more into my gift, my creativity flourished. I could write and talk about unbound all day. Women resonated deeply with the word. My email list doubled within a few months. Potential clients contacted me after reading just one article because my writing was speaking to them so compellingly.

Everything shifted. Because I was (and am) living in and from my gift.

There are three key lessons from my story that will help you to move more deeply into your own gift zone.

Lesson One: The difference between being in and outside your gift zone can be super-subtle

The unbound path is one of many subtleties and this is one of them. As you can see from my story, you can feel like you're completely in your gift zone, everything makes perfect sense logically and it can feel like all the parts are in place, BUT something is still sticking.

You can be right on the edge of your gift zone, you can be tapping on the window, soooo freaking close, but if you're not actually *in it* you'll find that life doesn't quite flow in the way you want to. (Nearly there is never enough for your Unbound Self).

It's obvious when you're miles away from your gift zone. When I was in finance, stuck in a corporate role, I knew I wasn't in my gift. I felt depressed, unmotivated and was continually seeking distractions. This may be where you are now? And if you are, celebrate.

Celebrate the fact that it's obvious to you that you're way outside your gift zone. Because when you're way outside, it's easier to make the decision to create change. Chances are that's why you've picked up this book? You're in a great position (even though it may not feel that way right now).

But when you're operating just outside your gift zone, it's not so easy to notice. Things may be ticking along okay, but deep down there's a nagging doubt that you're not quite being and bringing your full self to the world. Maybe you keep finding roadblocks in your path, getting sick or not making the money you'd truly like to?

Perhaps you can't seem to have the impact you really want to?

These are all signs you're outside of your gift zone. So even if things feel pretty good for you, even if you're just about there, know that making a subtle shift could make all the difference for you.

Lesson Two: You don't have to have it all figured out

Truly. You don't.

As a recovering good girl, I can understand the desire to have your path all mapped out, to know exactly where you're heading and what you're here to do in the world. This is why finding your purpose is such a big draw in the self-help world. We're all trying to get it right; to know.

But the truth is you learn through doing. You get to know where your gift zone is and how to move into it by experimenting, trying things out and (sorry to break it to you), making mistakes.

I know this might be tough to hear. Because we all want to cut to the chase, don't we? We all want to be there now. I get it.

But what if you simply chose to play with this idea? What if you decided to be curious, to take steps and notice what feels good and what doesn't, giving yourself permission to course-correct and love the journey, rather than obsessing about the destination?

I never would have discovered my unbound mission (or it would have taken a helluva time longer) if I hadn't started taking action before I knew where I was going. When I left my corporate job nearly ten years ago, I had no idea where I was heading. I had no clear idea what my gift was. I just began.

And this is an unbound quality I invite you to cultivate - to start before you know the full picture. As you tune into the inherent wisdom of your body and allow pleasure to be your compass, trust you will be guided along the way. Chances are you'll move into your gift zone sooner than you think.

Lesson Three: What comes easily to you has the most value

Something I've heard time and time again over the years is the fear that if something comes easily, it doesn't have value. So many of us have been brought up with the idea that anything of value has to come through hard work, that it's almost impossible to believe that in reality the complete opposite is true.

That thing that you couldn't stop yourself from doing if you tried? That thing that flows so easily that you lose yourself when you're doing it? That thing that comes so naturally to you, it feels almost effortless? That thing is your gift.

I can bet you don't completely believe me though. There's probably some kind of 'Yes, but...' coming up for you.

'Yes, but it can't be that easy.'

'Yes, but no-one would be interested in that.'

'Yes, but surely people wouldn't pay me for that?'

I get it. We've been taught that life has to be a struggle, so we tend to over-complicate things when it comes to finding our gift zone. We'll have a natural talent or skill, but rather than simply letting that come forth, we'll try and dress it up as something else, squeeze it into a neatly-labelled box, or continually sign-up for new trainings to try and seem more qualified.

Believe me, I'm a master at this. When I strip it back, my gift is to unbind women from their stuff. Women naturally unbind in my presence. I can see it happening.

But my Inner Good Girl doesn't believe that this is quite enough. She's the one who needs countless qualifications, a fancy website and endless content. She feels a need to justify her position.

My Unbound Self? She simply makes the offer, 'Come. Be. Unbind'.

The beautiful simplicity of that! I feel a glorious sense of expansion as I read it. How about you? What if you were to offer your gift in such a beautifully simple way?

So now, I invite you to strip back all of the complication and trying and clutter and ask yourself, 'What gift does my Unbound Self want to offer?'

Listen for the answer. And know that that's enough.

In fact, it's more than enough.

This is living in and from your gift.

The unbound woman thrives in sisterhood.

PRINCIPLE FOUR - SISTERHOOD

The fourth principle of living unbound is support and sisterhood. The unbound path can be a lonely one. If there's one thing I hear over and over again from the women in my unbound community, it's that often the people around them just don't get them.

In a world that values conformity and colouring between the lines, the unbound woman doesn't quite fit. She's the one who wants to go off travelling the world, home-school her kids, set up a communal living space or start a coven. None of this necessarily fits into societal expectations and the unbound woman can be judged as quirky at best. Often she's seen as awkward, difficult, lazy or just plain weird, even by those closest to her. She can end up feeling like there's something deeply wrong with her because she just doesn't fit.

Well, I can tell you now my friend, there is nothing wrong with you. You just haven't found your people yet.

The unbound woman needs her sisters around her. She needs to be amongst women who get her, who see her brilliance, who understand her desires and want to hear her true voice. The unbound woman thrives in sisterhood.

For the longest time, I resisted this. I had an embedded belief that I had to handle life's challenges on my own. Like many women, I was closed off to asking for or receiving support.

But the truth is when we allow ourselves to be seen and heard as we truly are, something magical happens. It's like breathing a beautiful sigh of relief, our bodies relax, a chink appears in the armour we've been accumulating our whole lives, a lightening, a softening; it feels like floating in a warm ocean of acceptance, completely supported and free to move in any direction.

The support of sisterhood opens up infinite possibilities.

I've experienced the power of sisterhood time and time again. When I host a retreat or run a workshop, at the beginning of the experience it can feel like the barriers are up. The women who have stepped forward to take part are unsure of what's coming next, protective and sometimes guarded. As the day or days unfold and each woman begins to share her truth, her vulnerabilities and her gifts, an incredible shift happens. I've seen women enter an event like this, looking closed off and tense, and by the end of the experience, they look completely transformed; relaxed and radiant.

This happens each time a woman allows herself to bathe in the energy of being witnessed as she truly is and witnessing the same in other women. It's one of the most healing and transformational experiences there is.

When we come together, we become more; we become more of who we truly are.

But as I mentioned above, often we can resist coming together in sisterhood. And there is a reason for this. From a very young age women can be conditioned to believe a concoction of poisonous stories which leave them feeling confused and ambivalent about the idea of sisterhood.

Let me share with you some of the main myths that could be standing in the way of you connecting with other unbound women.

The Myth That You Need to Sacrifice Your Own Needs to Support Other Women

This first myth means that many of us have the idea that being within a group of women will drain our energy in some way. I'm sure we've all experienced that dynamic in the past, either within a group of friends or work colleagues, at a workshop or on a course. You can end up feeling like you're supporting everyone else and receiving nothing back. Or you spend the whole time listening to other women bitching and complaining about how things are for them, leaving you feeling depleted rather than uplifted.

This can also happen in one-to-one friendships, where you feel like you're always the one in the supporting role and the relationship has become out of balance.

This can come up when I connect with women who are considering stepping into one of my group coaching programs or retreats. Often there's a concern that being within the group environment will be draining for them.

I get this. I've always felt more comfortable in one-to-one situations myself. And I know that part of this is the fear that my energy will be diffused by being within a group (as well as some other, more insidious reasons which I'll get to shortly).

But the truth is that this draining dynamic often arises because of the deeply ingrained belief that most women carry that other's needs are more important than our own. As little girls, most of us are brought up to be the nurturers, the caretakers, the ones who look after others. So, when we become adults, we continue to take that role in our friendships and other connections.

We sacrifice our own needs to meet the needs of others because we've been taught to.

And this plays out in groups of women, over and over again, often leaving individuals within those groups feeling either resentful that they've given too much or guilty that they haven't given enough. Double-bind anyone?

Our work as unbound women is to shatter this old belief and find ways to be in community that uplift, rather than drain; ways that leave us feeling lit up, rather than downtrodden; ways that make us feel more, rather than less.

All of this is possible. And it begins with you.

Start to notice the way you feel about coming together in groups with other women. Is there a part of you that resists this because you feel you're going to have to give more than you have to give?

Send some love to that part of you now. Let her know that her fears are based on old stories that don't have to be true. Let her know that you're willing to create a new way and you'd like her to help you.

Resolve to connect with other women in a way that feels expansive. Set your intention to fill up on sisterhood in a way that serves everyone.

Just shifting your perspective here will make a big difference. Each time you come together with other women, use this as your mantra:

As I connect with and uplift you,
I connect more deeply with and uplift myself.

Let's move onto the next myth that can make us resist sisterhood.

The Myth That Other Women Are
Our Competition

The idea that we need to compete with other women is one of the patriarchy's most pernicious lies. Again, from an early age we receive the mixed messages that although good girls should play nicely, be friendly and look after each other, you also need to watch out because the other girls may be prettier, cleverer, more popular and talented than you.

The media pedals the idea that *other* women are out to get your man, bitch about you to your friends, take that promotion you've been dreaming of, steal your best ideas and slyly put you down behind your back or to your face. And maybe you've had these kinds of experiences? I'm sure all of us have felt burned in some way in our relationships with other women. I hear these kinds of stories over and over again from the women in my community when I'm talking about sisterhood.

'Yes, but Nicola, this is what happened to me...'

It's no wonder we get so confused about female friendships! On one hand we feel a pull to be with other women and on the other we have a fear of being betrayed, or hurt, or abandoned. And this fear often comes from painful experience.

So, we hold back.

We compare ourselves to others and fall for the bullshit story that if she has more, then I must have less.

But the truth is, any experiences of feeling betrayed by other women often come from the fact that we've each internalised the patriarchal idea that other women are out to get us in some way. So, it can feel easier and safer to cause hurt in another, rather than to be on the receiving end at some point down the line. Simply recognising this in yourself and in other women can be incredibly healing.

We've also been conditioned to pull other women down, rather than to lift them up and celebrate their successes. I notice this in myself. When I hear about another woman thriving, or doing something that I'd like to do, rather than automatically wanting to send her a high-five, I can slip into envy or jealousy. 'Why can't I have what she's got?' Not an attractive trait I know. But it stems from that belief that there's not enough to go around and other women are somehow out to take from you.

It's time for this to change.

The unbound woman believes that a rising tide lifts all ships. When one of us thrives, we all benefit. Rather than falling for the scarcity myth that if she has more, there's less for me, what about creating a new story that says, when she has more, so do I. How does that feel?

I know it might feel alien at first. There might be times when you succumb to the green-eyed monster. And that's okay. There's no judgement here and it certainly doesn't help if you start giving yourself a hard time in any way.

Simply notice how you feel in relation to the other women in your life, both in-person and online. Experiment with celebrating each of their successes.

Whenever you start to feel resentful or jealous of another woman's life, see this as helpful information. You're being shown something that you'd like to create for yourself. (You wouldn't feel resentful or jealous otherwise). So, celebrate this new information. And then celebrate her.

Write a different story about sisterhood.

Change the old patterns.

Forge a new way.

And to help with that, let me share an even more destructive myth that makes it impossible for us to be comfortable in groups of other women.

The Myth That Being in Sisterhood Will Get Me Killed

Okay, I know this sounds dramatic. I almost didn't want to share this one. But just think back for a moment. Have you ever been in a group of women and experienced a full body urge to get out and run away?

I know I have. Many times.

And this used to freak me out. I thought there must be something deeply wrong with me. My fear of being with other women seemed to be hugely out of proportion for me. I've generally had good experiences when I've been in groups of women. So, this urge to run seemed crazy.

But then I started to read more about the witch trials of the past, what have been called the burning times, when women were tortured and forced to turn against each other in order to save themselves.

Friend against friend.

Sister against sister.

Daughter against mother.

And as I worked on my own intermittent and disproportionate fear of being in circle with women, I recognised that this mortal fear came from a combination of past life, ancestral and collective wounds. These are wounds that many of us carry. Because the truth is that if you're an unbound woman, you most likely were and are a witch, a potently magical being.

And because of that you may also be carrying this profound and paralysing fear of coming together with other women. At a deep and subconscious level, the concept of sisterhood feels life-threatening.

This is why it's so incredibly healing and transformative to be in a group with other women, to acknowledge any fears that arise, to recognise the witch wound, and to create a new story about the power of sisterhood.

So, if you've ever felt a freaky and disproportionate fear of being with other women, know that you're not alone. Be open to the possibility that this could be something you're carrying from long ago, something that doesn't necessarily belong to you in this lifetime. And begin to create a new pathway for yourself.

You can do this by letting go of these old, deep fears. An approach that I recommend for past life or ancestral wounds such as these is EFT Matrix Reimprinting and you can find more details in the resources section at the end of this book. However, often just recognising and acknowledging that these fears may not relate to this lifetime can create a profound shift in itself.

The second way to create a new pathway is to allow yourself to be in circle with other women, to acknowledge any fears that come up around this and to move through them in community. This can be immensely healing. You might decide to start your own group or to join some kind of existing circle, either online or offline. Always take an attitude of curiosity and experimentation with you. Be gentle with yourself. And know that you are growing your sisterhood muscle.

The poet, Robert Frost, said 'The only way out is through'. This could be the mantra for the unbound woman. And I believe that it's especially true when it comes to sisterhood. Many of us are carrying scars around our relationships with other women. But rather than retreating into our shells and allowing ourselves to be isolated, what if we chose to be brave, to be on the ones who create new circles of women, who invite deeper connection with our unbound sisters?

Yes, we'll probably get scarred again. It will take time to let go of the damaging, patriarchal conditioning we've all been brought up with. But isn't it worth it? Isn't it worth the risk in order to create new ways for ourselves, for our sisters, for our mothers and our daughters?

I think so.

When the wildest storm is raging,
And others are looking for shelter indoors,
The unbound woman puts on her hat,
coat and boots,
And goes outside to be at one with
the elements.

PRINCIPLE FIVE - SHADOW

The fifth principle of living unbound is the alchemy of shadow integration. What I mean by this is a commitment to bringing what's currently unconscious into your awareness; shining a light on whatever has been repressed or pushed down or hidden or disapproved of or pushed away. Shadow work involves bringing any of those aspects of us that we've previously judged as wrong into the light and accepting, allowing, and celebrating it all.

In these pages I've been talking a lot about the conditioning we take on throughout our lives and these ideas about who and how we should be can cause us to push away different parts of ourselves. In the section on pleasure I wrote about how we can receive the message that enjoying our bodies is wrong and this can make us disown our sensual power, pushing it into the shadows. You might have taken on the idea that any sort of chaos or messiness is bad, so you push those aspects of yourself away and try to project a perfect image. Perhaps you feel reluctant to show your ambition, your weirdness or your wild heart?

Most of us are only willing to show what we believe to be acceptable and we do our best to hide everything else.

But it's in the 'everything else' that the magic lies.

When you are operating under the illusion that you have to be and behave in a certain way to be loved and approved of, you expend a huge amount of energy keeping yourself in check. And this doesn't just happen consciously. We've often made countless unconscious decisions throughout our lives about what's acceptable and what's not. This means there's a whole lot of trying to keep everything in place going on under the surface.

And if we do allow any of this perceived unacceptable-ness to bubble up to the surface, if we let our guard down and show some anger or judgment or messiness, we beat ourselves up afterwards (which again demands a huge amount of energy).

Imagine what would happen if we allowed ourselves to be exactly who we are, without this continual sense of judgement or self-monitoring?

The energy freed up to be channelled elsewhere would be incredible.

When you are making a part (or parts) of you wrong, either consciously or unconsciously, you are limiting your magic. Those parts of you that you've been made to believe are unattractive, unacceptable or unlovable are actually where your freedom lies.

The unbound woman embraces it all.

Maybe you're not completely convinced though? Because when you've spent most of your life trying to hide certain aspects of yourself and micro-managing your experience, then it can take a great deal of faith and trust to start allowing your full self out to play.

I get it.

For years I consciously and unconsciously strove to portray the image of the quintessential good girl. I thought I needed to be seen as sensible, responsible and hard-working. (Those words don't exactly feel magical, do they?) I did my best to hide the parts of me that were sloth-like, angry, clumsy or quirky. I was only prepared to show a limited range of myself. And it was exhausting.

I bound myself. And if I blew my top or failed in some way, I berated myself endlessly afterwards.

For me there was a very clear line between what was acceptable and what was not. And if I let my guard slip, I believed the consequences would be crazy high.

What I realise now is that a part of me, a very young part of me, had made the decision that unless I was being a good girl, I was unlovable. (In fact, this young part of me believed that even if I *was* being the good girl, I was pretty much unlovable anyway. Hence, I couldn't win.)

So, I held myself back in so many different ways, I didn't know which way to turn. I was basically tied up in knots of my own making.

The underlying reason for this is that it only felt safe for me to show certain parts of myself. I believed that when I was doing this, people couldn't criticise me (although of course they still could). I thought I had a greater chance of being loved if I moulded myself in a certain way (particularly by deeply inappropriate men as it turns out).

But whatever you push down ends up running you. And you can end up attracting precisely what you don't want. Huh?

So how do you bring your shadow qualities out into the light? When we've spent so long trying to hide parts of ourselves, we can forget they exist. Fortunately, there is a relatively simple and particularly unbound way of remembering your full self and I'm going to share it with you now.

The Shadow Work of the Body

Most shadow integration work involves exploring the recesses of the subconscious mind. The aim is to uncover, shine a light on and accept those emotions, beliefs and desires that we've previously suppressed.

However, there is a part of us that's neglected in traditional shadow work and that is the physical body. The truth is there is as much material to be explored in the physical realm as there is in the emotional and psychological realms.

As I've been affirming throughout these pages, in our quest to be truly unbound, we can't afford to neglect our incredible and sometimes challenging physical bodies. After all, we have each chosen to be incarnated in this lifetime in a human body, but for many of us with a strong interest in spiritual and personal growth, we often pay little attention to the vessels we've been born into; the vessels we're here to express ourselves through.

I'm sure you've heard the words, 'We are not human beings having a spiritual experience. We are spiritual beings having a human experience', from philosopher Pierre Teilhard de Chardin. And maybe you breathed a sigh of relief when you first heard that? Perhaps you never truly felt like you belonged here? So being assured of your true spiritual nature helped you to make sense of what you're doing on this ever more chaotic and confusing planet, with a bunch of people who generally seem to be flailing around as much as you are.

But the fact is, the limitless spiritual being you are has chosen to have this physical experience; to fully know what it means to be human, to live within and through a body. So rather than running away from your physicality and all the messiness, confusion and sometimes pain this entails, I believe your job here is to move more and more deeply into the human being you are. By moving into deep agreement with all aspects of your physical experience, you can gain access to a boundless well of energy, power, acceptance and love.

What are you scared to show? What parts of you are you hiding? I'm talking about physical rather than personality traits here. Because the body will give us vital clues about the qualities we don't feel comfortable with, the qualities we feel shame around, the qualities we've forgotten we even have, the qualities that have spent too long lurking in the shadows.

Let me go first. Like many women, at different times in my life I've been ashamed of many (if not most) parts of my body. But it all starts with my left ear.

My Left Ear

Yes, my left ear. It sticks out and is completely asymmetrical to my far neater, better behaved, right ear. I've always been conscious of my left ear and have tried to hide it with my hair. Even when I put my hair up, I make sure there are strands covering it.

Then last year I saw a post on Facebook. It was from a journalist looking for women with big ears who felt self-conscious of them and tried to hide them with their hair. The photo attached to the post was of Dumbo. (I'm not even kidding). And I immediately recognised myself as I read that post.

In that moment I realised that after all the personal development work I'd done and for all my talk of being our fullest, most authentic, unbound selves, here I had been trying to hide a part of me.

I reflected on how whenever I was making a video (usually spreading the unbound message ironically), my hand would drift up unconsciously to my left ear, making sure it was safely covered.

Hiding a part of me I felt ashamed of.

I was literally keeping my left ear in the shadows.

I started to wonder, how could my ear provoke such shame?

And the answer came immediately, because it stands out. It won't sit nice and snug. It doesn't try and fit in.

My left ear had something to tell me. She was being brought to my attention for a reason. And all of a sudden, after all those years of hiding her, trying to pretend she wasn't there, I was ready to listen.

What did she want to say to me?

Again, the answer came. (As the answer always does when you ask a question and listen).

'Show me! Show your quirks. Show your full self. I am powerful. Like an antenna. I am where your magic lies'.

I understood. And I wondered, what would it be like to actually show my ear?

I started to consciously tuck my hair behind my ear when I was walking down the street. I noticed when my hand habitually drifted up to cover my ear and let her show.

As I did this, I felt free. I felt a release; release from years of chronic self-judgement; a release from years of worrying about someone seeing this part of me I'd made wrong.

Because, really, it's just an ear!

But of course, for years it wasn't 'just an ear'. For years my left ear represented all those parts of me that felt different, weird, clumsy, ugly and shameful.

So, to let her show felt powerful. Even though no-one else probably noticed, the act of showing my ear unleashed something within me; a desire to be truly visible, to let my full self be seen; for me to truly love and accept ALL of me, not just the parts I feel are okay, but the parts I feel uncomfortable about too.

This process (inspired by a post on Facebook and a photo of Dumbo) made me realise that when we show those parts of us we've previously hidden, when we let them out into the light, it frees a huge amount of energy. Space appears. It feels like a huge sigh of relief. Finally! Another layer gone.

Lighter.

Freer.

More energised.

I realised that my left ear is a metaphor for all the parts of us that make us unique. And if we acknowledge the alchemy of shadow integration, we understand that the very parts we want to hide and suppress, are those places where our magic lies.

And What Else?

So, I started to journal on the other parts of my body I had shamed and tried to hide over the years. What did these parts of me represent? Here's what I came up with. (And this is by no means an exhaustive list).

My frizzy hair. Unruly and untamable.

My thighs. Chunky, substantial and sensual.

My right eye. (As if to counteract my left, sticky-out ear, my right eye has a tendency to shrink and look decidedly squinty, especially when I smile and especially when I'm having a photo taken). Asymmetrical and lopsided.

The dark hair on my forearms. My wild, animal nature.

My grey hairs. Wisdom, ageing, the crone.

My belly. Prominent, abundant, feminine.

My breasts. Asymmetrical, different, mismatching.

My smell. Potent, feminine.

There's a lot around asymmetry here, isn't there? And also, of shaming the unbound feminine parts of me - my wild, untamed nature, my potency, my deep wisdom, my sensuality.

When we do this shadow work of the body, it uncovers the parts of us that we've felt unable to accept, allow and approve of. And as we send this (often unconscious) disapproval to parts of ourselves as individuals, this is reflected in society at large.

Deeply Flawed

When I first started my business, I had a hypnotherapy practice and women would come to me for help with losing weight. I can't tell you how many times I looked at the woman sitting opposite me and thought, you don't need this. You look great. But of course, that wouldn't have helped. Even when I reflected these women's gorgeousness back to them, it wouldn't stick. Because we're all masters at deflecting compliments, aren't we? We bat them away without a thought, knowing they couldn't possibly be true. And how do we know they couldn't be true? Because only we know how truly, deeply flawed we really are.

Most of us are walking around with the secret belief that there is actually something very wrong with us. So, compliments just can't make their way through to us. However, criticisms or subtle suggestions that we may not be completely perfect, land easily. They shoot straight through to our most vulnerable spaces and make their home there; oozing their poison out into our souls for years to come.

Can you imagine how draining it is for each of us to carry around this heavy load of self-criticism and loathing? No wonder many of us have created emotional, psychological and physical barriers to try and protect ourselves. And these barriers often manifest as additional weight, particularly around the belly.

You know, when I used to work with women in my hypnotherapy practice around weight loss, I sometimes used to feel that this wasn't the best work I could be doing. To be honest, I used to feel a bit snooty about it, because a big part of me wanted to work with more spiritual issues. Now, as I write this, I can see quite clearly that there is no more important work than to help women, and myself, to come into deep agreement with the body we have chosen to live through in this lifetime.

There is no more important work you can do than to move into a place of radical acceptance of your incredible, physical body.

Because when we're out of agreement, when we're making any or most of our bodies wrong, this demands a huge amount of energy. This resistance is what leaves us feeling constantly tired, dissatisfied and striving for something other. This is what's stopping you from being truly free. These self-judgements are the ties that have been binding you.

Over to You

So, unbound one, it's your turn. What parts of your body have you been consciously or unconsciously shaming?

Take some time to reflect on this. Move through your body, from your head to your toes and notice how you feel about each part of you.

What parts of you do you not feel comfortable showing?

What parts of you have you been trying to change?

What parts of you have been criticised by others?

What do these parts of you symbolise?

What would it be like to send acceptance and approval to these neglected parts of you?

How could you begin to bring forth the qualities you have been pushing away up until now?

Be gentle with yourself here. It could be easy to slip into judging yourself for the way you've been judging yourself up until now. (And that's a downwards spiral of self-criticism that no-one would benefit from!)

Remember we only push parts of ourselves into the shadows that we believe are unworthy, unacceptable, not enough, too much or unlovable. And we didn't come into the world with these beliefs; we've picked them up along the way.

From a very early age, we're taught to judge ourselves and others. It's hardwired into our existence. So, the work you're doing here is much-needed and pioneering.

Turn your gentle attention to your body. Be curious about how you feel about different parts of you. Welcome any insights that bubble up. And know that awareness is the first step to freedom.

PART TWO

THE CHALLENGES OF LIVING UNBOUND

The unbound woman embraces it ALL.

Okay, I'm guessing you might be thinking, 'Nicola! You've already been talking about plenty of challenges that come with living unbound. Surely there can't be more?'

I hear you.

And like I said at the beginning of these pages, the unbound path is a heroine's journey. You can absolutely avoid these challenges by slinking back to the familiar. No-one will judge you for that.

But you didn't come here for that, did you? You didn't come here to stay in the illusory safety of the familiar. You came here to be fully expressed, free and freaking magnificent.

So, before you start the next section, I invite you to see each of these challenges as an opportunity to step more fully into your personal power. If there's one thing I've learned very clearly over the past few years in particular, it's that we learn and grow most quickly through challenge.

Alchemy can emerge from anarchy.

Magic happens in the muck.

So dive in.

Your Unbound Self is right here with you.

And we start with her twisted and magical sister - the Bound Self.

The unbound woman gives space and deep approval to the many, unique and deliciously diverse parts of her.

THE BOUND SELF

As I explored what it meant for me personally to be unbound, I had one of those realisations that can change everything. I was journaling on what it's like to live an unbound life and as I tuned into the essence of me that is expansive, abundant and boundless, I recognised that there is also a part of me that actually wants to be restricted, tied down and limited.

There must be. Because otherwise I'd be experiencing complete boundlessness in my life. And I'm quite clearly not.

I have times when I feel deliciously unbound, expansive and free.

I also have times when I feel bound by my circumstances; times when I feel limited by finances, times when I feel misunderstood and invisible, times when I feel stressed and anxious and times when I feel that the door to a particular opportunity is firmly shut in my face.

And if having is evidence of wanting (as one of my favourite teachers, Carolyn Elliott, so eloquently suggests), then a part of me must *want* to be bound.

Although this idea was shocking to me initially, as I journaled on the idea of the Bound Self, I began to understand her motivations.

We all say we want to be free, to live a life with no restrictions or limitations, but the truth is that freedom comes with a whole host of complications – the need to take radical personal responsibility, to make (often challenging) choices, to decide what we *really* want and to claim it.

None of this is easy. Particularly when you haven't been encouraged to live an unbound life by your family, your schooling and society in general.

How much easier it is to do what you're told, to let someone else take responsibility, to allow yourself to be moulded by someone else's desires?

But there's more to the Bound Self than simply wanting to stay safe and stick with the pack. In contrast to the Inner Good Girl, who wants to please others and is externally motivated, the Bound Self is purely internally motivated. She's like the Inner Good Girl's edgier, stranger and more powerful, older sister.

She wants to be bound because it feels good.

She enjoys the feeling of limitation.

Paradoxically, there's something freeing for her about being tied down.

She appreciates the sensations of restriction and the drama of having few or no choices.

She savours it all.

And you might be reading this saying, 'No, that's not me. I don't have a part of me that enjoys being bound'.

I understand.

This is an uncomfortably confronting idea. But I invite you to reflect on your life and notice whether there's a particular area (or areas) where your Bound Self is showing up.

Maybe it's staying in a corporate job where you feel like you're sacrificing your true self?

Perhaps it's the way you've built your business, which means you're stuck doing things in a more masculine, linear way that leaves you feeling dead inside?

Maybe it's staying in a relationship where you're not able to express yourself fully, leaving you feeling stifled and frustrated?

There are endless ways the Bound Self can manifest her shadowy desires. She's potently magical. And she gets her energy from the fact that we don't tend to recognise or acknowledge her.

We endlessly strive for freedom and feel frustrated when we come up against limitation.

We focus on getting out of the box, rather than wondering if we could possibly enjoy the sensations of curling up within it.

And in doing this, we deny our Bound Self. We make her wrong. We shame her.

That's why we keep finding ourselves in the same painful patterns of limitation and scarcity. Because the Bound Self is unconsciously beavering away under the surface.

So, what do we do to change this programming?

The answer is very simple. And also very challenging.

We let the Bound Self come out to play. We give her some space. We acknowledge and honour her.

When we give approval to the Bound Self, when we allow her to enjoy the limitation she's created (rather than shaming her for it), she doesn't have to work so hard. Everything frees up. And a ton of energy is released. (Once again, this is something I learned from my fellow unbound woman, Carolyn Elliott, and her practice of Existential Kink).

Let me give you an example of how I've allowed my Bound Self to experience the pleasure of limitation.

Recently I set an intention to bring a certain amount of money into my business by the end of the month. As part of this, and in line with traditional Law of Attraction techniques, I allowed myself to get excited about what it would feel like to reach my expansive money goal. Doing this met the needs of my Unbound Self.

Then, to acknowledge the unconscious, shadowy desires of my Bound Self, I allowed myself to also imagine what it would be like if I made NO money in my business that month. And rather than sliding into panic about this, I let myself get excited about this possibility too – the shame, the drama, the feeling of restriction. I knew my Bound Self would love it and I spent some time allowing her to enjoy these feelings.

Obviously, this doesn't tie in with the traditional Law of Attraction teachings, because you're giving energy to something you don't consciously want. But the fact is that if there is any kind of limitation showing up in your life right now, then there is an unconscious desire for this. Your Bound Self will be at play whether you acknowledge her or not.

And, of course, it's not easy to give approval to the Bound Self. Because we're not taught to allow or even acknowledge these kind of shadowy desires (although it's likely you will see evidence of their manifestations all around you). This is a practice and it can take time to move into a place of approval towards the Bound Self. (And when you do, this feeling of approval may be fleeting).

But whenever you do access a feeling of approval towards her, even if it's just momentary, something magical happens. You stop being attached to what you *believe* you want, your conscious desires, and enter that transformational (and elusive) place of true non-resistance.

This is the alchemy of shadow integration.

And this is a key challenge for the unbound woman. We can't just try to put a lid on all of our shadowy desires. To experience true freedom, we have to acknowledge and accept all the many, unique and varied parts of us and the experiences we're creating in our lives. I'll share more about this later in the book in the section on high potency practices. In the meantime, I know that the idea of the Bound Self can be mind-twisting, so let me ask you some questions that will help you to explore what I've talked about in this chapter for yourself.

What would it be like to invite your Bound Self into your awareness? What does she look like? How does she move? What does she want you to know?

Look back on your life. Are there particular areas where it feels like your Bound Self has been at play? What was it that she desired in these situations?

What does it feel like to acknowledge your Bound Self? How does she respond to being acknowledged?

The unbound woman recognises that in order to know, we must first allow ourselves to not know.

SITTING IN THE VOID

One of the big challenges for an unbound woman is building a tolerance for sitting in the void. What is the void? It's that in-between place we return to after action, at the completion of a project and following an ending of any kind.

The void is a place of not knowing. It's not clear what will come next. It's often a place of rest and restoration. And it takes a great deal of trust to reside here. Because most of us have been conditioned to stay busy. As I talked about in the section on harnessing the power of your cyclical nature, we're not taught to honour the ebbs and flows of energy that we experience. We're taught to push on through and make it happen. Rather than allowing yourself to be guided by your pleasure, working in alignment with your cycle, and being in your gift, you end up trying to force it.

If that's you or if you notice yourself trying to force certain things to happen, please know that we all do. We all fall into this pushing and striving at times, because this is what we've been conditioned to do. This is what we've been brought up to do. Our whole educational system is based on pushing and striving. So, it's no surprise that many of us fall into this pitfall. But to walk the unbound path you need to start carving a new way. And this involves building a tolerance for spending time in the void.

The void tests us because it demands that we sit with a feeling of uncertainty, not knowing what comes next. This can be deeply uncomfortable and therefore the tendency is to rush through it.

It can feel so much easier to skip the void completely, to go up into your head and simply decide what's going to happen next. Why spend time feeling uncomfortable and not knowing when you can move on through to a more socially acceptable stage of the cycle?

The answer to this is that although being in the void can be frustrating, it is also a magical place. When you allow yourself to take time in the void, it leaves space for your Unbound Self to uncover the most potent next step of your journey. It's a place of percolation, integration, unconscious processing, that is deeply necessary. But because it feels like nothing is happening, the urge to move straight back into action can be overwhelming.

It can feel completely counterintuitive to sit in the void, particularly if you're not feeling where you want to be in your life, your business, your relationships or your career. There can be this strong urge to just push and make it happen, and mould things into place to make it right.

But if you allow yourself to just be in this place of not knowing, if you allow yourself to have this space, you get to stop jumping into things that take you further away from yourself.

Things like calling that guy you're not really lit up about, because you're uncomfortable being on your own.

Taking the first job that's offered to you, even though you know it's likely to sap your soul, because you feel guilty and panicked about not working.

Deciding to move ahead on a project that doesn't feel quite right, because you feel more comfortable being in action.

All of these are completely understandable examples of jumping out of the void. They're also examples of veering off the unbound path and further away from your true self. And sometimes you don't even realise that you've moved further away from yourself until you're way down the line. You have this moment of "Oh shit! Why did I even start this in the first place?" I'm sure we've all experienced that. We've all made decisions from a place of pushing and striving, and the fact is they can impact us for weeks or months or years afterwards. I know I've certainly made decisions where the repercussions have lasted for years and I've ended up in a situation that I *really* didn't want to be in. Whereas if you allow yourself to take this time in the void, then you gain true insight into your next steps.

As a recovering good girl, I know about the urge to action only too well. In a world where busy-ness is a badge of honour, it takes courage to stop, to say, 'Actually I don't know what comes next and I'm taking the time to allow this to emerge'.

I used to feel like there was something deeply wrong with me whenever I found myself in the void. I would flail around desperately trying to decide what was my logical next step. I would battle against the not knowing. It felt completely counterintuitive to simply allow myself to be there, to be present with my unknowingness. I didn't realise this was actually a key part of the creative process.

In order to fully know, we must first allow ourselves to not know.

When we try and force knowing, we limit ourselves; we end up creating from the bound, rather than the unbound.

This is why the unbound woman needs to learn to recognise and reside in the void. At first this will feel unfamiliar and uncomfortable. Every part of you may be screaming at you to move. Keep reminding yourself that this is a vital stage of the creative cycle of your life.

Affirm to yourself, 'I choose to relish my not knowing'.

The void is a place of immense possibility. Allow yourself to be excited by this rather than fearful. As Fritz Perls said, 'Fear is excitement without breath'.

Enjoy the muddiness of this creative, liminal space.

Trust that so much is happening under the surface, magic that you could never fully imagine or control.

And as you recognise this as a vital part of the cycle, know that you can't help but move through it at some point; that someday the clouds will part and the sunlight of clarity and inspiration will warm your face again.

And so it is unbound one.

The unbound woman knows that she is blazing a trail and creating a brand new normal for herself and all the women who will be inspired by her.

THE UNEXPECTED GUILT OF FREEDOM

If I were to ask 100 people whether they wanted more freedom in their lives, the majority of them would probably answer, 'Hell yes!' But the sad truth is that most of those 100 people probably wouldn't be willing to do what it takes to actually create more freedom for themselves - following the principles of living unbound, letting go of what no longer serves, recognising and changing the unconscious conditioning that keeps us bound.

Most people pay lip service to freedom. And I used to be one of them. Because the truth is creating true freedom, being truly unbound, is bloody hard work. You have to commit to making real change and there are countless challenges along the way.

When you start to walk the unbound path and allow more freedom in your life, you will stand out. You will stand out because most people are NOT walking the unbound path. Most people are stuck in the bound place, living a restrictive half-life and putting up with situations that feel pretty darn mediocre at best.

And this is their choice. (Because we all have a choice).

But as you start to create more and more freedom for yourself, something unexpected can happen. You can start to feel a creeping sense of guilt.

This guilt arises because it's not easy to be the one going your own way when everyone else around you is still following the expected path.

It's not easy to be the one who's allowing pleasure to be your compass when everyone else is being guided by obligation.

It's not easy to be the one who's living in beautiful alignment with your cyclical nature, following the ebbs and flows of your energy and inspiration, when everyone else is stuck working a 9-5.

So, you might start to look at the people around you and think, 'Surely it can't be right that I'm getting to live unbound, whilst they're stuck in a corporate job they hate/with a guy or gal who squashes their magnificence/working all the hours trying to make it happen?' You start to feel guilty because you're not fitting into the conditioned way of being.

For example, let's say as part of your unbound life you've created a schedule where you have an abundance of space and freedom. Now as we know, being is not celebrated in our culture. Doing is. So, having an excess of 'free' time can feel decidedly unusual and somewhat alienating.

'Surely I should be doing something?'

'Surely I should be working harder?'

These are the kind of questions you might find herself pondering upon. Because you've consciously created a life where it's not all go, go, go. As an unbound woman, you desire time and space and that's exactly what you've given yourself.

But a part of you can feel guilty about this.

It's the same guilt you might feel if you were playing hooky from school or taking a sick day from work.

You see everyone else rushing around doing lots of 'stuff' (most of which they clearly don't enjoy) whereas you are wandering through the park, appreciating the warmth of the sun on your skin and experiencing the stunning richness of each moment.

'Hmmm, surely this can't be right?' You might think to yourself.

I get it. Because I've experienced this guilt many times as I've walked the unbound path. If you've read my first book, Heal Your Inner Good Girl, you'll know that I used to feel super-defensive when Mr H would joke that I was living 'the life of Riley' when he went off to his corporate job each day. I felt a need to justify myself, to prove that I was working hard too, that I was a productive member of society. And this need came from guilt.

I can feel this guilt creeping up when I'm talking to friends who are stuck in situations they don't enjoy, situations they downright hate. And this guilt can lead to a tendency to hold back and not share the unbound-ness I've created in my life.

That's why it's SO important to keep reminding ourselves that we have chosen the unbound path. We are consciously creating a new way which is certainly not easy and has its own set of unique challenges. Often the unbound woman needs an excess of time and space to expand and tune into the insights that lead to these new ways of being.

One of the things that my clients often say when they start working with me is that they don't have role models who are creating an unbound life in their particular industry or area. This is a fact. There really aren't many unbound role models right now. So we need to be the role models.

Whenever you feel that guilty feeling starting to pull you down into self-doubt, remind yourself of this: You are blazing a trail and creating a brand new normal, both for yourself and for all the other women who will be inspired by you (and they will be).

When you create more freedom in your own life, you're not just doing this for yourself. The impact of your unbound-ness will ripple out into the world around you and into the collective. So, there's nothing for you to feel guilty about unbound one. Know that you are activating and inspiring others at every step, even if that's not immediately obvious.

The unbound woman is committed to taking radical personal responsibility for every single aspect of her life.

RADICAL RESPONSIBILITY

I've spoken a lot in these pages about how we're conditioned to behave in a certain way. Many of us were brought up to follow a familiar path: school, work, relationship, mortgage, family, retirement. And although that familiar path can feel restrictive, it can also feel beautifully comfortable.

When I think back to the days when I had a 9-5, there was something deeply soothing about knowing what I would be doing Monday to Friday and 48 weeks out of the year. Yes, I often felt frustrated and limited and unhappy, but I didn't have to expend time and energy wondering, 'Hmmm, what shall I do next? What do I really want? What direction shall I go in? How can I be my fullest self?'

Instead, I would generally be thinking about where to go for lunch each day, which way to walk home from work and where to spend my four weeks of holiday each year.

I'm being a little flippant there. Of course, I thought about what I really wanted to do with my life when I was in my corporate job. I felt restricted a lot of the time and deep down I knew that I wanted to do something different. But I didn't have to think about it too much. Because I was cosy in the familiar schedule of the corporate world.

I knew how I would be spending my time each day.

I knew how much money would be deposited into my bank account at the end of each month.

And I could easily plan ahead. I knew what I would be doing next week, next month, next year.

You can see how that could be soothing, can't you? Or maybe the right word is 'numbing?'

Now I run my own business I have so many more choices. Each day can look very different. I get to choose what I do and when. I get to choose what projects I focus on next, who I collaborate with and how I work with my clients. I get to choose whether to work at all. And as I've created a location-independent business, I get to choose where I'm based.

I'm continually confronted with choices. Because that's what freedom is: the ability to make choices about how you live your life. And this involves taking radical personal responsibility for your life and the choices you make.

The very nature of living unbound is that it's limitless. So, the unbound woman doesn't get to relax up and fall into the familiar. She's continually asking herself 'What do I really want?', tuning into her true desires and allowing herself to be guided by pleasure.

When we're following the familiar path, we don't have to take full responsibility for our choices. We can blame our situation on someone else or maintain, that 'It's just the way it is'. (How many times have you said or heard that?)

'Oh, I couldn't have done anything different'.

'I had to do it'.

'There was no way out'.

There's a great deal of safety and relief in this perceived restriction.

Whereas when you're following the unbound path, anything goes. You take full responsibility for your actions. Whatever you do, it is your choice. And you must own it.

'I choose this'.

Say those words out loud now. 'I choose this. I have chosen this. This is my choice'.

Notice how that feels.

Choice is powerful and freeing and scary.

Living unbound opens up doors of possibility, doors to the unknown, doors to the previously unimaginable.

The old, familiar structures fall away. And this can leave you feeling exposed. You don't get to hide behind what everyone else is doing. You're not one of the herd any more. Taking radical responsibility for your life means that you're off on your own and because of this you're going to stand out.

Your choices will be noticed. And that's a wonderful thing, because you're showing the way to other unbound women.

Your choices will be noticed. And that's a terrifying thing, as you open yourself up to ridicule, to criticism, to misunderstanding, to confusion, to feeling like you've failed and having to start over.

Freedom is messy.

Creation is chaotic.

When we make unbound choices, often they don't turn out as we expected. (Because where would be the fun in that?)

Taking radical responsibility can lead us in unexpected (and often unapproved of) directions. And make no mistake, this can feel deeply uncomfortable to the people around you too. The very fact that you're exercising your divine right to choose how you show up in the world can trigger the fuck out of those who are stuck in the familiar.

Every time you make a choice about who and how to be in this life, you reflect back to anyone who's feeling stuck or restricted or limited their disempowerment. And that will piss people off.

This the price of being a way-shower, a path-finder, a freedom-seeker.

The unbound woman is committed to taking radical personal responsibility for every single aspect of her life. She does not shy away from difficult decisions.

So, yes, figuring out what you want and actually making choices based on that can be challenging, but it also allows you to be the magnificent being that you truly are. Worth the discomfort? I think so.

The unbound woman recognises and accepts that she is a paradox.

HOLDING THE PARADOX

The unbound woman recognises and accepts that life is inherently paradoxical. She has learned that she is able to hold two seemingly opposing ideas or emotions at the same time. And, more importantly, she has given herself permission to do so.

Whereas the Inner Good Girl likes to have everything cut and dried, black and white, with clear, unwavering opinions, the Unbound Woman allows herself to change her mind, to move fluidly from one point of view to another and to contradict herself, sometimes within the same sentence.

And of course, this can be a challenge. As an unbound woman you may well be judged as flaky, muddled or crazy by other people. You may be told that you don't make sense. (And believe me, as an unbound woman who's married to a super-logical engineer, I've been told this MANY times!) The people around you may become frustrated with your seemingly contradictory, shape-shifting qualities. But that's because they're not able to recognise the paradoxes that lie within them; the paradoxes that lie within all of us.

The Unbound Woman does.

And she is.

A paradox.

But an even bigger challenge than the way other people perceive us can be the way we judge ourselves for the continually changing landscape of our minds and emotions.

I was at an event with Regena Thomashauer, author of Pussy: A Reclamation, when she made this simple, but immensely powerful statement:

'Woman doesn't make sense, she makes truth.'

Amen. I felt something free up within me as I heard these words.

Because how many times have you been told you don't make sense? And how many times have you told yourself the very same thing? When you're in the depths of emotion, moving between grief and uncontrollable giggles, rage and ecstatic joy; 'This makes NO sense'.

At these times it's important to remember that the feminine leads with emotion, rather than plain logic. She is open to the duality of life. She has a felt sense of this duality each month as she moves through her cycle.

So yes, I am sad and angry.

I am wildly creative and logical.

I am shy and extroverted.

I am boldly sexy and reticent.

I am brave and terrified.

I know that I am all and nothing.

I value both fierce connection and boundless freedom.

I am playful and deeply serious.

I am flippant and respectful.

I am supremely confident and hugely self-doubting.

When we allow it ALL, rather than expecting ourselves to have a defined, consistent way of being, we grant ourselves immense freedom. And only we can give ourselves this permission to allow it all.

As an unbound woman you see that any ideas of 'right' and 'wrong' are an illusion. So, you don't get to sit back smugly on the 'I'm right' train. You have to continually tune into what feels good for you right now. And then carve your unique path accordingly.

To help with this, ask yourself the question, 'What is my truth right now?" Journal or speak out loud to this. Let the words flow.

You can also use the prompt: 'Right now I am ......' and see what comes through for you.

At unbound workshops and retreats, I often invite attendees to do this in pairs. One woman asks, 'What are you?' over and over again, as her partner answers with whatever comes to mind.

- 'What are you?'
  'I am nervous.'

- 'What are you?'
  'I am a daughter'.

- 'What are you?'
  'I am a warrior'.

- 'What are you?'
  'I am grieving'.

- What are you?
  'I am bubbling over...'

It's incredible how often the most beautiful and profound paradoxes emerge during this exercise and to have these witnessed is powerful and healing.

So, unbound one, never deny or doubt your paradoxes. Acknowledge, accept and own them. Because this is where your power and freedom lie.

The unbound woman is committed to being potently magical.

The unbound woman is committed to her
potential happy.

PART THREE
HIGH POTENCY PRACTICES FOR
LIVING UNBOUND

So, I've given you the five principles of living unbound and I've talked a lot about the challenges you will experience on the unbound path.

Hopefully you've got the picture that showing up as your truest, most magnificent, unbound self is important, not just for you, but for the world. And I want to make sure you feel supported in doing that.

So, in this final section I'm sharing six practices that will help you to maintain a state of high potency. Now when I say 'high potency', I don't mean being in a state of constant action. Being at your most potent will sometimes look like taking a nap, going for a walk or spending time in the void.

These practices will enable you to feel more present in your experience, to experiment with what if means for you to be unbound and to feel beautifully supported as you carve your own unique, unbound path.

The unbound woman knows that everything is unfolding perfectly.

PRACTICE ONE - DEEP AGREEMENT

A high potency practice that relates strongly to the alchemy of shadow integration is deep agreement. This is the act of asking yourself, 'How can I move into deep agreement with where I am right now?'

The practice of deep agreement is based on the idea that all suffering is caused by resistance to what is. Resistance is the gap between what you believe you want and your current experience. This perceived gap can cause frustration, disappointment, anger, jealousy, sadness, longing, self-loathing. Jeez, the gap is NOT fun.

When we become aware of how we're experiencing the gap, we can also consciously choose to close it.

I realised this very clearly when out for a walk one Easter, in Rochester, upstate New York. It was a Friday in mid-April and it was snowing. I was pissed off. I was cold and irritated. The sky was grey. I had to wear my big winter coat, hat, gloves and boots. And really, I wanted to be walking in warm, Spring sunshine. I wanted blue skies and birdsong. I wanted to be wearing sandals and summery dresses. I wanted to feel the warmth of the sun on my skin.

I want.

I want.

I want.

And, of course, in that moment I was focused on all the things I didn't have. Which was in no way whatsoever helping my mood. Funny that.

So, I noticed what I was doing. I noticed how my thoughts weren't exactly uplifting me. And this question popped into my mind:

'What if I could be in deep agreement with where I am right now?'

Mmmmm.

What if I could choose to be in deep agreement with the cold and the snow and my big winter coat?

Even the act of asking the question felt good. Something relaxed within me. I felt soothed. The gap was closing.

What if I chose to appreciate what I have, rather than focusing on something different?

Deep agreement.

Just the words felt like a delicious sigh.

Deep agreement.

Like snuggling under the duvet with a loved one.

Deep agreement.

Bringing myself back to where I am, rather than wishing for something other.

That wishing. Oh, that wishing and wanting and striving. That pushing and trying and thinking. The gap.

Quite honestly, it brings tears to my eyes when I recognise how much of my life I've spent effort-ing and trying to make things different. And I'm pretty sure it's been the same for you. But what if we could allow ourselves to experience deep agreement?

Of course, this is not what we're generally encouraged to do. From the moment we first become aware, we learn that doing things a certain way helps us to gain approval. First at home, then at school, at work, at play. Everywhere.

Do it like THIS.

Be like THIS.

You need THIS.

Always THIS. Always something other.

And when you reach one THIS, another one immediately rises up to take its place.

Endless THIS.

So, we end up missing what's already here.

This body.

This life.

This love.

This moment.

The practice of deep agreement is learning to bring your attention back, to let your eyes wander lovingly over your current experience.

Your current feelings.

Your current thoughts.

Your current home.

Your current relationships.

Breathe into it.

And let yourself be here.

How does that feel?

Let me give you another example to show how deep agreement can work in practice. As I'm writing this now, I'm thinking back to when I woke up early this morning and experienced an irrational pang of fear. Deep in my belly. A clenching.

Fear of what? I don't know. And my first instinct was to push it away, because my conscious mind was telling me I shouldn't feel scared.

'Try to focus on something different Nicola. Move your attention elsewhere.' And then, I had the awareness that this trying was simply creating more discomfort. I was making my current experience wrong.

So instead I asked: "What if I could be in deep agreement with this fear?'

A softening.

What if I could move towards this feeling, rather than running away?

Hmmm. Moving towards fear? Let's see.

I brought my attention to the physical sensations I had labelled as fear. I moved my awareness down into my belly. I felt the clenching. I explored where it began and where it ended.

I stayed with it and nuzzled up alongside this fearful sensation.

'I agree with you', I whispered. 'I'm here with you. I honour you. I accept you. Welcome'.

And just like that I drifted off back to sleep. I allowed my mind to stop whirring. I moved towards myself. I closed the gap. And when you close the gap, you make space for something new to emerge.

And I know this doesn't make a lot of sense. In Gestalt theory, they call it the Paradoxical Nature of Change. 'Change occurs when one becomes what she is, not when she tries to become what she is not'.

The first time I heard about this theory, it opened something up within me. A recognition that all of those years of pushing and trying weren't the answer. A knowing.

And, of course, I forget this time and time again. My Inner Good Girl kicks in, some new self-improvement plan is created, and my attention moves to 'over there'. The key is to recognise those times when we're defaulting to being in disagreement with ourselves and our experience (which is likely to be a lot of the time!) and to consciously bring ourselves back into deep agreement. To do this, you simply need to ask the question, 'How could I be in deep agreement with where I am right now?' And notice what happens.

You will usually experience some kind of softening, a relaxing, like something being let go. But there will likely also be times when you feel more frustrated when you ask this question, times when you think the question is just stupid and how could you possibly be in deep agreement anyway?

It's all good. Like everything else in this section, this is a practice. So, experiment with it.

And hold your experience lightly unbound one.

The unbound woman sees discipline and structure as ways of serving the Divine in a more powerful way.

PRACTICE TWO - DIVINE DISCIPLINE

I'll admit, I've never liked the word 'discipline'. To me it has always suggested someone forcing some kind of regime on me, as if I'm being made to do something which involves suffering.

In fact, the dictionary definition of 'discipline' is:

'The practice of training people to obey rules or a code of behaviour, using punishment to correct disobedience.'

Eurgh! Those words have me running for the hills. And as an unbound woman, I'm guessing that you probably feel the same?

But as I reflect on what it takes to be the most potently magical I can be, I realise that there *is* room for discipline in my life. Now, please don't throw the book down in disgust at the very thought of this! Bear with me, as I'm about to explain my reasoning.

The truth is that in order to be unbound, to be our fullest, most powerful and magnificent selves, we need some kind of structure to support us. We need the many and varied parts of us to be operating at their fullest potential. And when we don't have any structure in our lives, our potency can become diffused, draining away into the ether without making the impact we desire.

So, it's time for a reframe about discipline. And we can do that by thinking about discipline as divine.

What I mean by this is rather than thinking about discipline as simply being in service to ourselves, or to some other person we're trying to please, we begin to see discipline as being in service to something other, to the Divine, to the animating source of all that is.

When I started to re-imagine discipline in this way, I felt activated rather than oppressed.

Something within me wanted to commit, to give of myself and to serve something greater. This was not about sticking to some external set of rules, but rather creating a code for myself, a code that would allow me to be all I can be.

Just take a moment and notice how the idea of divine discipline feels to you? Imagine how it would be to make a commitment to some kind of action or practice in service to the Divine, rather than doing it because you feel you should or because someone else told you to. What happens to your body when you shift your thinking around discipline in that way?

I'm guessing you will experience a softening, an expansion, a sense of purposeful power that infuses every cell within you. Pretty good, huh?

When I initially tuned into the idea of divine discipline, my first act was to commit to walking for two hours each day for thirty days. I knew that this would be a high potency practice for me and I also knew that it would demand discipline. It's a stretch. I love walking but taking two hours out of every day was a big commitment (particularly on days when I was busy with clients or when it was raining for the whole two hours I was out walking!)

But thinking about this being in service to the Divine kept me on track. This practice became something that was non-negotiable for me. As I began each walk, I dedicated it to the part of me that desired spaciousness, to the Goddess and to Mother Earth. The whole act felt sacred, rather than something I was pushing myself to do. And this 30-day commitment fed me in so many ways. It created space and structure in my days, I got to connect with nature, I felt more creative and physically strong. And throughout all of this I was making a powerful offering to the Divine.

When we think about discipline as divine, it's no longer a dirty word, something to be resisted. It becomes something that you actively want to invite more of into your life, because you know that it makes you infinitely more magical. Divine discipline is very much one of the high potency practices that will serve you as you move forwards on your own unique unbound path.

As with everything unbound, the way we perceive things is key. As an unbound woman, you need to find ways to be at your most potent without feeling that you're sacrificing any of your freedom. This can be a subtle balancing act, as I've found both personally and through working with my clients. The words we choose, the way we choose to relate to the world within and around us, the way we see ourselves – these are all a part of the spells we are casting on ourselves moment to moment. And we cast those spells either consciously or unconsciously.

As you can see from what I've written here, the difference between something feeling like it's constricting or expansive can be very subtle. Living unbound demands that we're continually reflecting on our intentions for taking any particular course of action. I could very easily have done my 30-day walking practice and been up in my head the whole time, going over my to-do list in my mind and rushing to get back to my desk. This would have been the very same act, a two-hour walk each day, but it wouldn't have been at all spacious, magical or unbound. By bringing my focus back to my intention, to make an offering to the Divine, I created a daily practice that felt truly spacious, freeing, deeply connecting and creative. Now I'm not saying I didn't have times when I was up in my head, thinking about what I could or should be doing as I was walking. I certainly did! But when I noticed this happening, I simply brought myself back to my intention and the divine nature of my walk. Each time this moved me out of any draining 'should' energy and back to the awareness that I was doing something sacred.

So, can you begin to re-imagine your relationship with discipline? (Because, I'm taking a guess that you've resisted it in the past).

Here are some questions that will help you to reflect on this more deeply:

What have my experiences of discipline been in the past? How could I choose to reclaim my relationship with discipline in order to be at my most potently magical?

What do I feel called to offer up in service to the Divine? What could be part of my personal divine discipline practice? (Maybe this could be something related to one of the five principles of living unbound? Perhaps you could start a specific practice related to following your pleasure, being aligned with your cyclical nature, living in your gift, bringing your shadow into the light or stepping into more sisterhood?)

Where am I feeling stuck or stalled in my life and/or business right now? In what subtle way could I choose to see this differently? What words could I use that would allow me to feel more powerful?

The unbound woman is
energised by mystery.

PRACTICE THREE - CONSCIOUS SECRET KEEPING

Let's face it, secrecy is not something that's generally encouraged. Secrets tend to be associated with shame, something that needs to be hidden. We've all had (or have) secrets like this and you can feel how they drain your energy.

However, there is a type of secret that can be energising. A secret that you choose to keep, just for yourself. Not because you have to, but because you want to.

In this era of social media and radical openness, there is little kept hidden or mysterious. There's an urge, an expectation even, to share everything that happens to us on a daily basis. But there's often little thought as to whether this sharing is energising or draining. When we feel the need to habitually share, share, share, it diffuses our energy.

I remember an experience when I was travelling in Peru. It was before the days of social media, but still most people were taking lots of photos and so was I. I wanted to document my journey, so I could share the photos with friends and family and look back at them myself. But there was one guy who didn't have a camera. When I spoke to him he said he had made a conscious decision not to take photos during his trip. He wanted to be fully in the moment and he wanted that moment to be just for him.

This was unusual back then, but it would be even more surprising now in the Instagram age of sharing every detail of our day. And I'm not against sharing. It can build connection and community. But when we're sharing continually, or feel like we should be sharing continually, our energy is being directed outwards.

Conscious secrets can bring that energy back.

As I talked about in the last chapter, a few months ago I started an experimental practice of walking for two hours every day for 30 days. My initial impulse when I got the idea was to document and share the process with my online community. But I very soon realised that I wanted to keep this experience just for me. The whole idea of this walking practice was to give myself space, to nurture the body, mind and spirit in a powerful way. I sensed that the potency of this practice would be lost, or at least diffused if I was sharing as I went.

So, I made a decision to keep this experiment secret. When I was out on my walks I didn't take my usual photos. Instead I chose to drink in each moment for myself. And this felt powerful.

Each of us has so many opportunities to share our experiences right now. This is a wonderful thing. But just because we have opportunities doesn't mean we have to use them all.

I come into contact with so many women who are passionate about changing the world, creating new ways and helping others, but many of them are getting burned out and feeling drained because they feel a pressure to be 'on' constantly and to be sharing with their communities daily. If you are one of these women, please know we need you to be at your most potently magical, not exhausted, run down and depleted.

One way you can stay potently magical is to experiment with the practice of conscious secret-keeping. Here are some questions to reflect on which will help you to get started:

Where are you diffusing your energy by sharing right now?

What project or idea are you working on that it would feel powerful to keep secret?

How do you feel about secrets in general?

The unbound woman recognises that unbound doesn't mean unboundaried.

PRACTICE FOUR - SACRED BOUNDARIES

Unbound doesn't mean unboundaried.

This has come up time and time again for me over the past few years, as I've personally dived deeper into what it takes to live an unbound life. And what I've discovered is that the boundaries we set for ourselves are the most important of all. Of course, we want and need to have clear boundaries around what's acceptable and unacceptable in our relationships with others, both personal and working. But it's just as, if not more important, to have strong boundaries around what we expect from ourselves.

When walking the unbound path, it's easy to slip into a 'go with the flow' kind of approach. Believe me, I have been the master of this! We crave freedom and when we get it, or when we choose to allow ourselves to have it, it can be hard to know where one part of our life starts and another ends. Work becomes play and play becomes work. One activity can have more than one intention.

For example, say I go for a walk which is part self-care, part exercise, part creativity, part meditation, part reflection, part working, part Facebook-living and part catching up with phone calls. This can be okay (and some of my walks may well be like this, depending on which stage of my cycle I'm in), but it can also feel muddy. Without clear intention, our power becomes diffused. We lose focus and any benefit we receive from a particular activity gets watered down.

The setting of personal boundaries can be very subtle, but it's vital. We need to create containers in order to harness and focus the power of our magic. Without a container, we have freedom but no potency. That can be fun, but if true creation is one of your aims (and I'm guessing it is, since you're here), then potency is key.

This became clear to me when I was doing some work with the different parts of myself and their seemingly conflicting desires. (This is work that I do regularly for myself and also with my unbound clients). There's a part of me that craves simplicity and spaciousness. She was neglected for a long time in my life. Like most of us I was brought up to value busy-ness and achievement. So, for many years I either ignored the part of me that desired space and a simple life or I squeezed her into small pockets of time - spa days, retreats or meditation classes.

There's also a part of me who craves stimulation. She wants to be fully engaged and to be taking powerful, creative action. If you looked at my life from the outside you would imagine that this part of me has had her needs met over the years. I've lived a full life. I've had a lot of different experiences. And I've created a great deal. But when I tuned into these different parts recently, I realised they required a very specific quality to their individual desires.

The part of me who wanted simplicity and spaciousness wanted this need to be met in a very particular way, which is actually difficult for me to put into words. I know this is not the most helpful thing for a writer to admit, but there's a subtlety to her desires, which I can feel but not necessarily describe to you.

The same applied to the part of me who desires creative stimulation and action. When I connected with her, it was clear that busy-ness was not enough. Her needs were about quality over quantity and again that quality was very specific.

For both of these parts it was clear that the potency of however I spent my time was key. So paying lip service to spaciousness or creative action simply wasn't going to cut it. They were telling me very clearly that I couldn't just phone in some time when I would just be or some time for creative action. I had to be fully present in whatever experience I was choosing.

Presence = potency.

As I was doing this work with my mentor, she mentioned that what was coming through from these parts didn't seem too different from what I was already doing in my life. And this is true. I've consciously created a life where I have a lot of space and also, I take a lot of creative action. So, you would think I had a double-tick there. But there was a different quality that needed to come through. And in order to achieve that quality, I needed to put some personal boundaries in place.

Rather than telling myself that I would just go with the flow, I live an unbound life, so I can do what I want from moment to moment, I needed to step up and be willing to move deeper into my experience.

This involved setting boundaries.

Sacred boundaries.

Boundaries that elevate.

For me this looked like creating some non-negotiables - a daily walk, meditation, two dedicated pockets of time each day where I would check social media and emails, distraction-free creative time, a commitment to finishing this book and not sharing for the sake of it.

Conscious.

Clear.

Potent.

So, how about you? What kind of boundaries could you put in place to elevate your experience? What needs to happen for you to feel more present in the different areas of your life?

This may mean letting go of some activities, obligations and relationships that no longer serve you.

It might mean putting clearer boundaries in place with people in your personal and work life.

It will very likely involve getting super-honest about the quality you bring to each area of your life and how you choose to meet the needs of the many and varied parts of yourself as an unbound woman.

Take a deep breath and ask the question: 'What are the sacred boundaries that I need to put in place right now in order to be my fullest, freest unbound self?'

Notice what comes to you. And trust the answers you receive.

Make it a part of your high potency practice to keep checking in around this and reflecting on your personal boundaries. Listen to your body. She will tell you when your boundaries are slipping, because you will find that you're feeling drained, anxious, tired or wired. And the next chapter will help you to tune into her wisdom more deeply.

The unbound woman realises that her body always knows.

PRACTICE FIVE - LEARNING TO LISTEN TO YOUR BODY

The very nature of being an unbound woman is that you create situations that can feel unsettling; You are an agent of questioning and change. And although this creates great possibility and freedom, it can also create discomfort. That is why we require the high potency practices I'm sharing here to support us. And learning to truly listen to your beautiful, wise and wonder-full body is one of the most important.

To listen to your body, you need to be IN your body. And this is not as easy as it sounds. As I wrote about in the section on pleasure, we're conditioned to move away from the wisdom of our bodies and operate from the mind. When it comes to walking the unbound path in the most potent way, this is just not going to cut it.

Your body knows. Always. And she will be able to guide you every step of your way if you allow her to. This is the practice.

In the year I was writing this book, one of my greatest unbound dreams came to fruition. I got to move from the UK to upstate New York with Mr H whilst also continuing to do the work I love. I was experiencing the laptop lifestyle I had heard about since I first became interested in creating an online business several years ago.

And the freedom and flexibility of geographical independence was a wonderful thing to experience. But there were also many challenges. As part of making this move to another country, Mr H and I went through a process of deep questioning of our marriage. Within two months of me making the move, both of my parents were diagnosed with serious illnesses. These diagnoses came one after the other, knocking our family to the core.

The reality of managing these kind of life events, whilst living an unbound life can be extremely challenging. It's certainly not all light, joy and unicorns. Choosing to live unbound puts you slap-bang in the path of uncertainty and sometimes chaos. So, it's important to have strategies and resources in place to help you feel grounded and centred in the face of life's curveballs.

My go-to practice has become tuning into my body, turning my attention away from the pushes and pulls of the outside world and my busy mind, going within and asking her, 'What do I need right now?'

As an example, when I got the news that my dad was sick, it was early on a Friday morning. I had been expecting it. He'd had an appointment with his consultant and this was the recurrence of an old problem. So, I was able to be relatively matter of fact when the news came.

I spoke to my sister and my parents. And then I tried to go about my day as normal. I went outside onto the porch to write my morning pages. This is usually a great grounding practice for me. But as I was writing, I realised I just didn't have the words.

This practice that usually helped me to feel more connected seemed to be detaching me from my experience. I felt like I was dancing around the surface, as I tried to put pen to paper. A sense came over me, an overwhelming urge to go inside, lie down, to close my eyes and breathe. To be. To be with my body and whatever was arising.

So, I did. I'm usually committed to writing my morning pages (because, divine discipline, right?), but I gave myself permission to stop half-way through and to lie down with myself. After many years of being the good girl and doing what was expected, this kind of unbound act of self-listening and self-care is revelatory. Every time I make a choice like this, I'm carving a new way for myself.

I was meant to be going camping that weekend. And not just any sort of camping. This was to be a proper, wild camping trip, hiking to the base of the highest peak in New York, setting up camp and then trekking up the mountain. We would be carrying whatever supplies we needed. There would be no convenient wash block or facilities. And I would be sleeping solely on a camping mat.

Usually the challenge of this experience and the idea of being outside in raw, untamed nature would be perfect for me. But as I listened to my body, I knew that I just couldn't do it that weekend.

I could feel my body saying a gentle but firm, 'No' to the idea of getting up at 5am to make the trip. She tensed and contracted at the thought of it.

So rather than pushing through (which would have been my old pattern), I told Mr H that I couldn't face making the camping trip that weekend. Instead we spent time together, talking and enjoying the surprisingly warm October weather. This choice was immediately healing. My body responded to the way I had listened to her by relaxing and opening up. I felt soothed.

And this is a practice. It takes time to build up a trusting relationship with your body (especially if you've been overriding her needs for years). When you begin to live by the principles of allowing pleasure to be your guide and living in alignment with your cyclical nature, you can't help but create a deeper connection with your body. You can't do either of these things from a mind level. You need to gently listen to the cues your physical sensations are giving you. So, you're already on the right track.

This specific practice is about continually coming back to your body with the question 'What do I need right now?' and (most importantly) listening and acting on the answer you receive. In doing this, you create a powerful bond with your physical self. And she will help to keep you anchored in even the most challenging of times.

So, try it out now, even if you're a pro at listening to the wisdom of your body (because we could all do with listening to her more often).

Take three deep breaths. Bring your attention down and away from your mind, into your body and ask the question: 'What do I need right now?'

Then listen.

Maybe you will receive a very clear answer. Or perhaps you will simply have a sense of what you need to do (or not do). Remember this is a practice, so if you don't feel you're getting much initially, keep going. Let your body know that you want to hear from her. Show her love and attention. Check in with her regularly. And send her deep appreciation when she gives you her guidance.

The unbound woman gives zero fucks about taking the most comfortable route and creating neat and tidy outcomes.

PRACTICE SIX - CONSCIOUS BINDING

Okay unbound one, I've left this high potency practice to last because it might seem completely counter-intuitive, so bear with me! Obviously, the whole point of living unbound is to be free of restrictions and limitations. So, what the heck do I mean by 'conscious binding'?

Well, throughout these pages I've been sharing both the joys and challenges of living unbound. And the paradox is that the very things that give us access to a deep well of joy as unbound women - freedom and a sense of limitless possibility - are also the things that can create the most challenge for us. When you're an unbound woman, you are in charge of your destiny, you're the captain of your ship and you get to choose. Yeah sister!

And when we invite unbound-ness into our lives, there can also be a great deal of uncertainty, upheaval and often chaos. And this is not necessarily created intentionally. Simply deciding to be unbound will send powerful ripples through your life. Your Unbound Self gives precisely zero fucks about taking the most comfortable route and getting neat and tidy outcomes. That's not what she's here for. So, when you welcome her into your life, she'll be there, playing full out and working her magic in the most powerful way. And this can feel like your whole life so far consists of mere crumbs on a picnic blanket that your Unbound Self is now shaking away with abandon to clear space for a sumptuous, new banquet. We all want the banquet, but it's no fun whilst those crumbs are being shaken away!

Within the first 18 months of making a commitment to live unbound, I experienced an unexpected move to another country, serious health issues with both of my parents, difficulties in my marriage due to prolonged times apart, the challenges of moving my business fully online and becoming location independent. And that's just the most major life events. There have been countless other minor(ish!) upheavals along the way.

This is why the practice of conscious binding is so vital.

As I wrote about in the section on the shadow work of the body, we have all made the decision to be bound in some way when we come into this life. The very nature of our physical, human existence is bound. And this is what we've chosen to come here and experience.

So, whilst living unbound, it's also important to honour this desire to experience the bound-ness of being human. In fact, it's only through our bindings that we learn to be truly unbound. And this becomes most powerful when we are conscious about it.

What do I mean by this? Well, conscious binding is the practice of becoming ultra-intentional about the way we choose to be bound (and recognising that this IS a choice).

Let me use my marriage as an example. To be honest, Mr H and I chose to get married because it was the logical next step for us in our relationship. We wanted to make a commitment to each other and to have a party for all our family and friends, so marriage seemed like a no-brainer.

But then I started doing all of this work around unbound and we got the opportunity to move from England to the US. This meant we ended up spending a lot of time apart, as initially Mr H made the move over to the States and I stayed in the UK whilst all the arrangements were made.

This period of separation led us to reflect more deeply on what it meant to be married. We're both highly independent and can easily be happy spending time apart. I began to question why I had chosen to bind myself to another person and the institution of marriage in this way. Wouldn't it be more expansive to be completely free?

Both of us spent time questioning our marriage. And we had many honest and challenging conversations around this. What we eventually realised was that although the freedom of being completely single and independent was appealing, our relationship brought a depth and richness to our lives that we wanted to maintain and grow.

For two people who've always felt the call of the unbound, making this commitment to be together, to stay together, to be consciously bound, felt powerful. We don't *have* to be together. We *choose* to be together.

This conscious binding feels supportive and anchoring. It creates a container within which we can both evolve and expand. By coming up against our edges, we learn more about ourselves, what we want to release and what we want to experience more of.

So a conscious binding has two important elements:

1) It's conscious, intentional. You recognise you have chosen it.

2) It creates a container that although it could be thought of as restrictive, through your intentionality it is infused with the ability to provide both support and anchoring, as well as the potential for growth.

Other examples of conscious binding could be: choosing to have children, any kind of relationship or friendship, caring for a family member or friend, having a pet, buying or renting a home, choosing a particular career or starting your own business.

All of these things may cause frustration, pain, boredom and limitation, but when we are very conscious about them, they have the potential to create growth, expansion and deeper levels of freedom.

This is the paradox of living unbound.

So, over to you.

Take some time to reflect on your current life. Are there any situations or relationships that have been feeling restrictive which you could begin to see as conscious binds? Is there a way that these experiences are supportive and anchoring to you? Are you open to the idea that you have chosen to experience this in order to come up against your edges and access a new potential for growth? How does that possibility feel for you?

Reflect on how you want to move forwards. Are there any possible conscious binds that you want to invite into your life? What situations or relationships could you move towards to in order to create a sense of support and anchoring, whilst also providing a potential container for you to come up against and grow through?

AFTERWORD

As I was coming to the end of writing UNBOUND, I took myself to the coffee shop in Rochester, New York where I had started the process nearly 14 months earlier.

I sat at the very same table with my mug of black coffee, took out my MacBook and started to go through everything I had written. The Beatles were playing in the background and I was completely absorbed in what I was doing. So when all of sudden someone plonked themselves in the seat opposite me, I was startled. As I looked across the table, it took me a few moments to realise it was a new friend I had made since coming to Rochester. We go to a yoga class together, but I hadn't recognised her immediately as this meeting out of context.

We hugged and chatted for a while. She asked what I was working on and I said I was in the finishing stages of writing my next book, UNBOUND. She asked what it was about, and I explained it was about being your truest self.

'But what if you're your true self and people don't like you?' she asked.

And as I reflected on her question, I realised that this is at the crux of making the decision to live unbound. As little girls most of us are made to believe that we have to be a particular way in order be liked. And we're also taught that being liked, being approved of and accepted, is pretty much the holy freaking grail when it comes to being a woman. Consequently, most of us have spent a huge amount of our lives trying to be liked.

Whatever else happens, I must be liked.

And when we have this idea that the most important thing we have to offer is our like-ability, this is when we end up stuck in situations that are deeply uncomfortable, restrictive and even dangerous. (#MeToo anyone?)

Goddess forbid you should be yourself, say what you actually mean, declare what you really want, and in the process make someone else feel uncomfortable or piss them off!

So, for this feisty, beautiful, intelligent and funny woman sat across from me in the coffee shop, when I talked about being your true self, her first thought was, 'Yes, but what if they don't like me?"

And of course, I get this. My Inner Good Girl still longs to be liked. Sometimes I catch myself holding back, modifying myself, agreeing when really I disagree, or laughing along when I actually feel uncomfortable. Lifetimes of conditioning don't get overturned in a few short years.

But my hope for you, for myself and for all women is that more and more, we can make being fully expressed our number one priority, rather than being liked.

Imagine if your daughter, your sister or your mother could cast off the shackles of like-ability, even just for a moment, and be her fullest, freest self.

This is how the world changes unbound one.

So, yes, when you're your true self some people may not like you. Because they are not your people.

Maybe you will find you no longer fit in that job you've been in for years? Because that's not what you're truly here to do.

Perhaps you will realise your relationship doesn't work when being likeable is no longer your main concern? Because this is not the love for you.

As I've said all along, being unbound is a heroine's journey. But I promise, when you commit to being your truest self, you WILL be supported.

You will be supported in ways you couldn't imagine.

So, as we come to the end of these pages, I honour you for being on the unbound path with me. Because this changes EVERYTHING.

Keep going unbound one. You're changing the world. And I'm right here with you.

Always, UNBOUND.

Nicola x

A PRAYER FOR THE
UNBOUND WOMAN

Dear Goddess, Divine Mother of all that is,

Today let me be free of the ties that have bound me,

Let me love the parts of me that are raw and dark and dirty and difficult,

Let me see my magnificence, even in the muck,

Let me know my connection with all things,

Let me love my wise and wild self,

And be in deep agreement with my experience, exactly as it is right now,

As I trust that everything is unfolding perfectly.

I fall into your fiercely nurturing arms,

And as I allow you to hold me, as you always have and always will,

I choose to let that feeling of being held to ripple out into all areas of my life, the life of all beings and the Universe.

I am.

And so it is.

Amen.

UNBOUND RESOURCES

Download your free UNBOUND bonus resources and continue the journey at:

www.nicolahumber.com/unbound-resources

Join the online community for unbound women at:

www.nicolahumber.com/unbound-collective

Recommended Reading for the Unbound Woman

Women Who Run With The Wolves by Clarissa Pinkola Estes

Pussy: A Reclamation by Regena Thomashauer

Slow Sex by Nicole Daedone

Code Red by Lisa Lister

Love Your Lady Landscape by Lisa Lister

WITCH by Lisa Lister

Red Moon by Miranda Gray

Sacred Retreat by Pia Orleane

Sacred Pleasure by Riane Eisler

A Return to Love by Marianne Williamson

The Desire Map by Danielle Laporte

The Big Leap by Gay Hendricks

The Pill: Are You Sure It's For You? by Jane Bennett and Alexandra Pope

Heal Your Inner Good Girl. A Guide to Living an Unbound Life by Nicola Humber

Find out more about EFT Matrix Reimprinting at:

www.matrixreimprinting.com

ACKNOWLEDGEMENTS

To Mark, my partner on the unbound path. Thank you for your support and questioning, for making me laugh (almost!) daily and for growing with me.

To Lou and Mani Bear, my unbound soul sisters. Thank you for the love and laughter, your endless support and a room of my own.

To Mum and Dad. Thank you for always being there, trips to and from the airport and your acceptance of all I am.

To my publisher, Sean Patrick of That Guy's House. Thank you for your ongoing support, for getting UNBOUND immediately, for seeing the witchiness in my words and encouraging me to embrace my inner Stevie Nicks!

To Clare Roche, my dear friend and mentor. I can't put into words how much you supported me during the writing of UNBOUND. Thank you for holding the most powerful space for me to find my voice.

To my fellow unbound women, friends, mentors and clients, who are on the path with me. Leah Kent, Carolyn Elliott, Carly Hope, Katie Brockhurst, Lyndsey Whiteside, Kate Gerry, Seanica Howe, Jessy Paston, Esther Copeman, Chetna Halai, Lisa Lister, Tanya Phillips, Ann Nilima Ruel, Sheila O'Driscoll and Simona Hamblet. You inspire and activate me more than you can know.

To Erin Kelly and Katrina Scarlett. Thank you for supporting me behind the scenes SO beautifully.

To Mary-Ann Lester and Angie Flack-Brown. Thank you for giving me a platform to share Heal Your Inner Good Girl and UNBOUND with the women of Rochester, NY. Your support means the world to me.

ABOUT THE AUTHOR

Nicola Humber is a leader of and mentor to unbound women everywhere. She activates recovering good girls to embrace their so-called imperfections and shake off the tyranny of 'shoulds', so they can be their fullest, most magnificent, unbound selves.

Nicola's first book, Heal Your Inner Good Girl, struck a chord with recovering good girls, helping them to cast off the shackles of perfectionism and people-pleasing, so they could create their own unique unbound lives. Her latest book, UNBOUND, takes us deeper into this journey of self-discovery.

Nicola has appeared on BBC Radio and written for the Huffington Post, Elephant Journal, Natural Health Magazine, Soul & Spirit, WITCH, Rebelle Society and Sivana.

Find out more about Nicola and her work at:

www.nicolahumber.com

Follow Nicola on social media at:

www.facebook.com/nicolahumber

www.instagram.com/nicolahumber

I'm a woman
Phenomenally.
Phenomenal woman.
That's me.
Maya Angelou

Lightning Source UK Ltd.
Milton Keynes UK
UKHW02f0528190618
324457UK00010B/530/P